Never Play Leapfrog with a Unicorn

Joella H. Mehrhof, Kathy Ermler, Vicki Worrell, and Joan Brewer

Address orders to: AAHPERD Publications, P.O. Box 385, Oxon Hill, MD 20750-0385,
call 1-800-321-0789, or order online at www.naspeinfo.org. Order Stock No. 304-10324

ISBN: 978-0-88314-925-6

Printed in the United States of America.

Suggested citation for this book:

Mehrhof, J. H., Ermler, K., Worrell, V., & Brewer, J. (2007). *Never play leapfrog with a unicorn*. Reston, VA: National Association for
Sport and Physical Education.

Table of Contents

Chapter 3: Moo May Represent an Idea, But Only the Cow Knows It

Chapter 6: A Bird Does Not Sing Because It Has an Answer; It Sings Because It Has a Song

OVERVIEW

Purring is the sound of a cat manufacturing cuteness. Let it be said that in the elementary school, cuteness does count, but it is not the only thing. Each day elementary school physical educators are allowed to guide students in learning skills and making choices that will improve their quality of life and extend their lifespan.

One of the strategies of accomplishing this feat is through quality, developmentally appropriate lessons based on student learning outcomes and national and state physical education content standards. The title of this book, *Never Play Leapfrog with a Unicorn*, is a humorous, but obvious example of an activity that is not appropriate for a physical education class. However, appropriate activity choices and teaching strategies to meet the content standards may not be as obvious.

The purpose of this book is to offer activity ideas for the K-5 elementary school physical education classroom that emphasize motor skills and movement patterns and to provide, through those activities, related ideas and methods to meet the national content standards.

Content Standards

The National Association for Sport and Physical Education (NASPE) has defined six physical education content standards that encompass the knowledge and skills necessary to allow students to emerge as physically educated individuals. The national standards for physical education provide the basis for student learning outcomes, as well as the assessment of the outcomes. These national standards are stated below.

Standard 1: A physically educated person demonstrates competency in motor skills and movement patterns needed to perform a variety of physical activities (skills and patterns).

Standard 2: A physically educated person demonstrates understanding of movement concepts, principles, strategies, and tactics as they apply to the learning and performance of physical activities (learning concepts).

Standard 3: A physically educated person participates regularly in physical activity (active participation).

Standard 4: A physically educated person achieves and maintains a health-enhancing level of physical fitness (physical fitness).

Standard 5: A physically educated person exhibits responsible personal and social behavior that respects self and others in physical activity settings (personal/social behavior).

Standard 6: A physically educated person values physical activity for health, enjoyment, challenge, self-expression, and/or social interaction (activity appreciation).

In each of the activities offered in this book, Standard 1 is emphasized. In addition, provided on each of the activity pages is information on how to focus on at least one other standard through a strategy alternative, an activity variation, or a concept adaptation. Across the bottom of each activity page is a ruler indicating which standards are addressed through the activity and its adaptations. For each activity, the ruler is similar to the one illustrated below.

Standard 1	Standard 2	Standard 3	Standard 4	Standard 5	Standard 6
Skills and patterns	Learning concepts	Active participation	Physical fitness	Personal/social behavior	Active appreciation

The shaded boxes on the ruler indicate those standards addressed in the particular activity. In the boxes below each standard on the ruler are shortened terms related to each standard.

Chapter Content

Chapter 1: *Never Play Leapfrog with a Unicorn*

This chapter relates the value of simple cues. Activities in which simple cues emphasize basic skills are offered. The cueing information for this chapter is provided in the "Leapfrogs" section found on each activity page.

Leapfrogs

Chapter 2: *Dogs Wag Their Tails with Their Hearts*

The students are ready to move (their tails are wagging!) the very second they enter the gym. This chapter emphasizes the importance of quickly, yet competently, beginning the learning process through the use of instant activity. A variety of instant activities and warm-ups are provided. The standards information for this chapter is provided in the "Bow WOWs" section found on each activity page.

Bow WOWs!

Chapter 3: *Moo May Represent an Idea, But Only the Cow Knows It*

This chapter offers activities that allow for the development of responsible student behavior. Often the physical educator expects certain behaviors, but has forgotten to relate these expectations to the students. Methods and activities for developing leadership, initiating team work, and creating a disciplined environment are offered. The standards information for this chapter is provided in the "Udder Things" section found on each activity page.

Udder Things

Chapter 4: *When You Have Got an Elephant by the Hind Leg, and He Is Trying to Run Away, It's Best to Let Him Run*

It is fairly easy to run (forgive the pun) with the idea of using the locomotor skills to teach and reinforce other physical education concepts. This chapter provides ways to take a single locomotor skill and change it into a group adventure, fitness activity, or partner challenge. The standards information for this chapter is provided in the "Forget Me Nots" section found on each activity page.

Forget Me Nots

Chapter 5: *If You Dance with a Bear, You'd Better Let Him Lead*

Throwing, catching, kicking, and dribbling are the basic skills that often dominate an elementary school physical education curriculum. In this chapter, those "bear" activities are approached through stimulating activities that allow for appropriate progressions, maximum participation, and fitness enhancement. The standards information for this chapter is provided in the "GRR-reat Ideas" section found on each activity page.

GRR-reat Ideas

Chapter 6: *A Bird Does Not Sing Because It Has an Answer; It Sings Because It Has a Song*

This chapter emphasizes the importance of rhythmic activities in a physical education curriculum. Many physical educators find teaching rhythmic activities to be an intimidating or at least uncomfortable task. Rhythmic activity ideas that approach the content from a simple, yet appropriate manner and allow the physical educator to "sing" his or her way through the rhythmic activity are included. The standards information for this chapter is provided in the "Tweet Beats" section found on each activity page.

Tweet Beats

Chapter 7: *It Is Impossible to Keep a Straight Face in the Presence of One or More Kittens*

This chapter offers ideas on incorporating fitness into other aspects of the physical education curriculum, as well as activities for developing and enhancing a high level of physical fitness. The physical educator will smile when students' faces are glowing from perspiration and beaming with the love of movement. The standards information for this chapter is provided in the "Cat Nips" section found on each activity page.

Cat Nips

Chapter 8: *When Putting Cheese in the Mousetrap, Always Leave Room for the Mouse*

This chapter examines the integration of other content areas (e.g., spelling, math) into the physical education curriculum while still maintaining a high level of physical activity and keeping the primary focus of learning on movement/fitness. The standards information for this chapter is provided in the "Gouda Ideas" section found on each activity page.

Gouda Ideas

CHAPTER 1

Never Play Leapfrog
with a Unicorn

Cues

Helpful Hints

Cues

• Cues should be short, simple, and to the point.

• Cues that help students visualize the motion are the best.

• Words are like a foreign language to beginners. Remember the expression, "What I hear, I forget. What I see, I remember. What I do, I know" (Confucius).

• In most cases, students need to actively practice the movement at the same time the teacher is showing the movement. Watching the teacher perform the skill does not help the students develop the skill. Have the students actively rehearse a skill in order to develop the initial kinesthetic sense.

• Too much instruction and verbal cueing is worse than no instruction. Try to find words that match the motion and use cue words that the students can repeat to themselves as they perform a skill.

• When giving students information about their performance, stick with the most critical error and focus on that error until it has been corrected. Do not give students too much information, just give them feedback on a way to modify the most critical error and then let them practice.

Jumping

Equipment Needs
Spot markers

- Have each student stand on one side of a line.

- Instruct the students on the cues of jumping:

    o Bend the knees and ankles before jumping.

    o Swing the arms backward and then forward at takeoff.

    o Take off on both feet and land on both feet.

    o Bend the knees upon landing.

- Have the students practice jumping over the line using the cues.

- Have each student place two spot markers a very short distance apart.

- Review the cues for jumping (i.e., bend, swing, jump, land).

- Have the students jump from the first spot marker to the other spot marker.

- After a few jumps, have the students increase the distance between the spot markers.

Leapfrogs

Jumping Cues

Bend

Swing

Jump

Land

Equipment Needs
Lummi sticks

Vertical Jumping

- To change from horizontal jumping to vertical jumping, have the students review the cues of jumping.

- The cues for vertical jumping are exactly the same except the arms reach forward and upward.

- Below are the cues for vertical jumping:

  o Bend the knees and ankles before jumping.
  o Swing the arms backward and then forward and upward at takeoff.
  o Take off on both feet and land on both feet.
  o Bend the knees on landing.

- Have the students practice vertical jumping.

- Have each student get a partner. Each pair needs one lummi stick.

- Have the partner with the lummi stick stand to the side and slightly to the front of the other partner. Have this partner hold the stick horizontally, away from the body, and at above-the-head height.

- Have the partner without the lummi stick practice jumping vertically in an attempt to touch the stick.

- After a few jumps, have the partners change roles.

Leapfrogs

Jumping Cues

Bend

Swing

Reach for the Stars

Jump

Land

Parachute Landing

Equipment Needs
Spot markers

- Jumping and landing must be taught together.

- Show the students how a person using a parachute lands (i.e., has soft knees, sinks slowly, lowers hands to the side).

- Give the students a verbal sound for sinking/lowering. An example might be "ahhhh" or "shhhhh."

- Have the students practice their parachute landing, including the verbal sounds.

- To begin a progression using this parachute concept, have the students begin walking in a confined space. When the teacher calls "parachute," the students demonstrate a parachute landing (no jumping).

- When the students have the concept of lowering the weight (parachute landing), have the students begin jogging in a confined space. When the teacher calls "parachute," the students quickly demonstrate the parachute landing (no jumping).

- To add the jump, have the students jump from one spot marker to another. Remind them to land using a parachute landing.

- To advance the progression, have the students jog around the area. When the teacher calls "parachute landing," the students run to a spot marker, jump and straddle the spot marker, and perform a parachute landing.

Leapfrogs

Landing Cues

Bend

Ahhhhhhh

Equipment Needs
None

Parachute Landing Practice

- Have the students practice jumping in various ways. Following are some sample jumping ideas. Remind the students to use the parachute landing.

  o Jump as high as possible.

  o Jump and land as quietly as possible.

  o Jump five times and stop.

  o Jump forward and then backward.

  o Jump side to side.

  o Jump, clap, jump, clap.

  o Jump over five lines.

  o Jump, jump, and turn.

  o Jump, land, and make a shape.

  o Do baby jumps.

  o Do giant jumps.

Leapfrogs

Jumping Cues	Landing Cues
Bend	**Bend**
Reach for the Stars	**Ahhhhhhh**
Jump	
Land	

Hopping

Equipment Needs
Spot markers

- Below are some cues for hopping:

  o Stand on one foot.

  o Shift the weight slightly to the standing leg.

  o Bend the knee of the standing leg.

  o Swing the arms backward and then forward and upward at takeoff.

  o Push off on one foot and land on the same foot.

  o Bend the knee on landing.

- To teach the locomotor skill of hopping, use colored spot markers.

- Have each student get two different colored spot markers to mark his or her position.

- Have the students stand on one foot on one of the spot markers.

- Instruct the students to bend the knee of the standing foot and push. A student should land back on the same colored spot marker on which he or she started.

- Be sure to practice on both legs.

Leapfrogs

Hopping Cues

Bend

Swing

Push

Land

Equipment Needs
Spot markers

Hop Trials

- Have the students practice hopping in various ways.
  Below are some sample hopping patterns.
  Remind the students to bend and push.

  o Hop 10 times on the right foot.

  o Hop 10 times on the left foot.

  o Hop twice on the right and then twice on the left foot.

  o Hop around the spot marker on one foot.

  o Hop on and off the spot marker three times.

  o Hop sideways onto the spot marker.

  o Hop backward onto the spot marker.

  o Hop three times and make a shape with the body.

  o Hop as high as possible and land on the spot marker.

  o Hop forward twice.

  o Hop forward twice and backward once.

Leapfrogs

Hopping Cues

Bend

Swing

Push

Land

Leaping

Equipment Needs
Spot markers

- Below are some cues for leaping:

  o Take a step with the planting foot.

  o Stretch forward and upward with the hands and forward with the leaping foot.

  o Lose momentary contact with the floor.

  o Land on the leaping foot.

  o Bend the knee when landing.

- To teach the locomotor skill of leaping, use colored spot markers.

- Have each student get two different colored spot markers to mark his or her position.

- Have the student stand behind the first spot marker and face the second spot marker.

- Have the student step onto the first spot marker and leap to the second spot marker. The student should land on the opposite foot. A leap goes from one foot to the other foot.

Leapfrogs

Leaping Cues

Step

Stretch

Land

Equipment Needs
None

Leap Trials

- Have the students practice leaping in various ways. Below are some sample leaping patterns. Remind the students to go from one foot to the other foot.

  o Leap three times in a row.

  o Leap down a line on the floor.

  o Do a hand motion while leaping.

  o Leap and clap on the landing.

  o Leap to the side.

  o Leap and make a shape on the landing.

  o Leap and make a shape with the body while in the air.

  o Leap as high as possible.

  o Run in a curved pathway and leap.

Leapfrogs

Leaping Cues

Step

Stretch

Land

Sliding

Equipment Needs
None

- To teach the locomotor skill of sliding, use the "Fox and Hound" concept.

- Show the students how "the fox is chased by the hound"— step to the side with the lead foot (fox) and bring the trailing foot (hound) up in a slight jump to meet the lead foot.

- Have the students hold one hand out to the side and point in that direction. This is the direction in which the chase goes. The students start with their feet together. The lead foot (fox) takes a step in the direction the hand is pointing. The trailing foot (hound) moves toward the lead foot by jumping slightly so that the feet are together in the air for a brief moment. Upon landing, the lead foot must still be heading in the direction the hand is pointing.

- To get the uneven rhythm of the slide, have the "chase" occur on a bumpy road. As soon as the students have the step-close pattern of the slide, instruct them to keep this motion going, but to pretend they are on a bumpy road. The students begin to get the up-and-down motion and the uneven rhythm of the slide by using this bumpy road concept.

- Be sure to practice sliding to the right and left.

Leapfrogs

Sliding Cues

Fox and Hound (step-close)
On a bumpy road

Equipment Needs
None

Galloping

- To teach the locomotor skill of galloping, use the "Horse and Buggy" concept.

- Show the students how the horse and buggy move— step forward with lead foot (horse) to a stride position and bring the trailing foot (buggy) up to meet the first foot.

- Have the students stand with feet together. Then take a step forward with the lead foot (horse).

- If the horse moves, so must the buggy, because they are attached. With that concept in mind, now move the trailing foot (buggy) toward the lead foot (horse) by rising slightly so that the feet are together in the air for a brief moment. Upon landing, the lead foot must be out front of the trailing foot.

- To get the uneven rhythm of the gallop, have the horse and buggy travel on a bumpy road. As soon as the students have the step-close pattern of the gallop, instruct them to keep this motion going, but to pretend they are on a bumpy road. The students begin to get the up-and-down motion and the uneven rhythm of the gallop by using this bumpy road concept.

- Be sure to let students practice the gallop using their other foot to lead.

Leapfrogs

Galloping Cues

Horse and Buggy (step-close)
On a bumpy road

Visiting Grandma

Equipment Needs
None

- Explain to the students that there are two ways to travel to Grandma's. They will either go by railroad (i.e., sliding) or horse and buggy (i.e., galloping).

- When the teacher calls "railroad," the students must find and stand on a line on the gym floor and begin performing the sliding motion.

- When the teacher calls "horse and buggy," the students use the galloping motion to travel anywhere in the area.

Leapfrogs

Galloping Cues	**Sliding Cues**
Horse and Buggy	**Fox and Hound**
On a bumpy road	**On a bumpy road**

Equipment Needs
Spot markers

Skipping

- Below are some cues for skipping:

    o Step with the right foot and hop on the right foot.

    o Step with the left foot and hop on the left foot.

- To teach the locomotor skill of skipping, have the students place spot markers in a large circle.

- Have each student start on a different spot marker and have them skip from spot to spot.

- A skip is really a step-hop in an uneven rhythm. In an attempt to get the uneven rhythm, tell the students to skip as if they are very happy. This idea will help with the lifting feeling necessary for the uneven rhythm of the skip.

- Have the students practice skipping forward and backward, as well as in straight and curved lines.

Leapfrogs

Skipping Cues

Step, hop, step, hop
Think happy

Iron Man Throwing

Equipment Needs
Throwing objects

- To teach students how to throw underhand using one hand, use the "Iron Man" stance.

- To get students in position for the "Iron Man" stance, ask them to stand facing forward with both feet on a line.

- Ask the students to indicate their throwing arms and have them take one step back from the line with the foot that is on the same side as the throwing arm.

- The students should all have one foot on the line and one foot behind the line. Once the students are in this position, tell them to bend their knees. This is the "Iron Man" stance (i.e., a stride stance with the knees bent).

- To throw underhand with a backswing, have the students start in the "Iron Man" stance. Have them bring their throwing arm behind them. Have them step forward with their front foot and swing the throwing arm forward to release a throwing object.

Leapfrogs

Underhand Throwing Cues

Iron Man stance
Up, up, and away

Equipment Needs
Spot markers

Muscle Man Stance

- To teach the overhand throw, use the "Muscle Man" stance.

- To get the students in the "Muscle Man" stance, have them place two spot markers on the floor about shoulder-width apart with their nonthrowing side (arm) closest to the target. The students put one foot on each spot marker and stand with their arms out to their sides at shoulder level. Bend the elbows to 90 degrees, bringing the fists up so that the palms are facing the sides of students' heads. The knees are slightly bent. This is the "Muscle Man" stance.

- To begin a throwing progression, have the students indicate their throwing arm. Have the students move the leg farthest away from their throwing arm back to where both feet are on one spot marker. This is the ready position (i.e., both feet on one spot marker).

- From the ready position, have the students step into the "Muscle Man" stance, rotate their bodies toward the target, and say "I."

- As the body begins to rotate and the head/eyes move to see where the throw will go, have the students say "want."

- As they continue the forward throwing motion, have them say "you" as they point forward (release the ball).

Leapfrogs

Overhand Throwing Cues

Ready position
Muscle Man stance
I want you

Muscle Man Throwing Practice

Equipment Needs
Throwing objects,
spot markers

- Have the students each get three soft throwing objects. Yarn balls work well because they are soft and do not fly very far.

- Have each student place two spot markers on the floor.

- Have the students begin in the ready position (i.e., two feet on one spot market).

- With one object in their throwing hands, the students step into the "Muscle Man" stance and rotate their bodies toward the target. The students say the "I want you" cue as they continue the forward throwing motion in order to throw the first object.

- Students can now practice this pattern with the other two throwing objects and then retrieve three different throwing objects. Repeat the throwing patterns.

Leapfrogs

Overhand Throwing Cues

Ready position
Muscle Man stance
I want you

Equipment Needs
Soft balls

Catching

- To teach the correct hand positions for catching, use the "Pinkie" and "Thumb" concepts.

- Demonstrate the "Pinkie" position for catching a ball below the waist (i.e., knees bent, leaning forward, palms up, pinkies together).

- Demonstrate the "Thumbs" position for catching the ball above the waist (i.e., knees bent, palms open, thumbs together).

- Tell the students to perform a certain locomotor skill in a determined area. When the students hear either the word "Pinkie" or "Thumb," the students immediately stop and get into the "Pinkie" or "Thumb" catching position.

- Play several rounds of this activity.

- Have the students get a soft throwing object and toss it to themselves so they can practice catching both above and below the waist.

- Emphasize that the students must move to get underneath the object.

Leapfrogs

Catching Cues

Pinkies (catching below the waist)
Thumbs (catching above the waist)

Pinkie Partners

- Have each student find a partner.

- Have each pair get a soft ball and stand four to five feet apart.

- Have the partners roll the ball to each other while practicing catching with their pinkies together.

- After the partners have completed several rounds of rolling the ball, have the partners toss the ball to each other below waist level.

- To progress, have each pair get another ball. Have each student roll a ball to his or her partner at the same time. When the partners can do this task successfully, have both partners toss (at below waist level) their balls at the same time.

- Continue to emphasize that the students may need to move to position themselves in front of the tossed ball.

Leapfrogs

Catching Cues

Pinkies (catching below the waist)
Thumbs (catching above the waist)

Equipment Needs
Soft balls

Thumb Partners

- Have each student find a partner.

- Have each pair get a soft ball and stand about four to five feet apart.

- The partners throw the ball to each other in order to practice catching with their thumbs together. Remind the students that the ball must be thrown so that it can be caught above the waist. Also, remind the students that they may need to move to position themselves under the tossed object in order to catch it.

- After the students have successfully caught several balls, try the following variations:

    o Have the receiving partner clap before catching the ball.

    o Have the receiving partner touch both elbows before catching the ball.

    o Have the thrower bounce the ball to the catcher.

    o Have the partners throw a ball to each other at the same time.

Leapfrogs

Catching Cues

Pinkies (catching below the waist)
Thumbs (catching above the waist)

Kicking

Equipment Needs
Soft kicking balls,
spot markers

- To teach the correct kicking position, use the "Shoelace" concept.

- Have each student get a spot marker and a soft kicking ball. Place the spot marker on the ground and put the ball beside and slightly in front of the spot marker. The ball should be placed on the kicking foot side of the spot marker.

- Have the students stand behind the spot marker and ball. Have the students step on the spot marker with their nonkicking foot and then brush the ball forward with the shoelaces (i.e., the top) of the kicking foot.

- When the students are successful with this kick, progress to a step-leap kick. Have the students stand a little farther behind the spot marker and ball. Have them step on their kicking leg and then leap to their nonkicking leg before kicking the ball.

- When the students are successful with this kick, progress to a momentum kick. Have the students back away from the ball and then run and leap to kick the ball. This movement pattern becomes very similar to a gallop.

Leapfrogs

Kicking Cues

Beginner Cue: Step, shoelaces

Intermediate Cue: Step, leap, shoelaces

Advanced Cue: Run, step, leap, kick

Equipment Needs
Soft kicking balls,
spot markers

Kick Backs

- Have each student get a ball and a spot marker and have them stand about 10 feet from the wall.

- The students place the spot marker on the floor and position the ball next to it. Practice kicking the ball at the wall. When the ball rebounds from the wall, have the students catch the ball and put it back beside the spot marker.

- When the students are successful at this task, have them stand behind the spot marker and roll the ball toward the wall. When the ball comes off the wall, have the students attempt to kick the moving ball back at the wall.

Leapfrogs

Kicking Cues

Beginner Cue: Step, shoelaces

Intermediate Cue: Step, leap, shoelaces

Advanced Cue: Run, step, leap, kick

CHAPTER 2

Dogs Wag Their Tails with Their Hearts

Instant Activities

All of the activities in this chapter meet Standard One (skills and patterns). Use the "Bow WOWs" to meet other standards.

Helpful Hints

Instant Activities

- Introduce a new instant activity as a part of lesson. After the activity has been introduced and fully understood, then that activity may be used as an instant activity that the students immediately perform as they enter the gym.

- Have a specific area in which the daily instant activities are posted. Make a sign stating the name of the day's instant activity. Post the sign in the instant activity area. Make the letters of the sign large enough so that students will be able to see it as soon as they enter the gym.

- Ensure that the instant activity relates to the skills used during that day's lesson. For example, if the students will be performing ball-handling skills during the lesson, have the instant activity include a ball.

- Instant activity time allows students to quickly enter the gym and begin learning. It provides the teacher time to take role, speak to the students, and even perform simple observational assessments.

Rock Star Throwing (Standard 1)

Equipment Needs
Balls, CD player, music

Appropriate for Grades K-2

• Have each student get a ball.

• While the music is playing, each student jogs and carries the ball around the activity area.

• When the music stops, the students stop to toss and catch their own ball until the music resumes.

• When the music starts, the students begin jogging again.

Bow WOWs!

The below adaptations address the additional standards indicated in the shaded boxes.

Standard 2: Ask the students what locomotor skill they will perform instead of jogging. Tell the students to use different trajectories, directions, and levels.

Standard 5: Do this activity with a partner. Allow the partners to take turns deciding what type of throw they will use.

Standard 1	Standard 2	Standard 3	Standard 4	Standard 5	Standard 6
Skills and patterns	Learning concepts	Active participation	Physical fitness	Personal/social behavior	Active appreciation

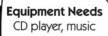

Equipment Needs
CD player, music

Stop, Drop, and Roll (Standard 1)

Appropriate for Grades K-2

- When the music is playing, the students use various locomotor movements to move around the activity area.

- When the music stops, the students stop, drop to the floor, and perform a log roll. This continues until the music begins again.

- When the music begins again, the students run in the opposite direction or use a different locomotor skill.

Bow WOWs!
The below adaptations address the additional standards indicated in the shaded boxes.

Standard 2: Have the students explain to a partner how to perform a log roll.

Standard 1	Standard 2	Standard 3	Standard 4	Standard 5	Standard 6
Skills and patterns	Learning concepts	Active participation	Physical fitness	Personal/social behavior	Active appreciation

Time's Up (Standard 1)

Equipment Needs
Watch or timer

Appropriate for Grades K–2

- Have all the students line up along the wide side of the playing area.

- Tell the students that they have a certain number of seconds to get to the other side of the area using a specific locomotor skill.

- For example, the students might have 15 seconds to skip across the area.

- On a signal, the students skip (or another called locomotor skill) across the area as the teacher counts.

- When the last number is reached, the teacher calls "Time's Up."

- A simple assessment can occur by doing this activity several times and viewing the students who are getting across in the allotted time. In addition, assessment can occur by watching the student perform the locomotor skills.

Bow WOWs!

The below adaptations address the additional standards indicated in the shaded boxes.

Standard 2: If a true 15 seconds was used, teach the students about pacing.

Standard 4: Reduce the count by one and have the students complete the same locomotor skill. Complete the task several times and have the students check their heart rate after each time across.

Standard 5: Have each student that crosses give another student a high-five as he or she completes the task.

Standard 1	Standard 2	Standard 3	Standard 4	Standard 5	Standard 6
Skills and patterns	Learning concepts	Active participation	Physical fitness	Personal/social behavior	Active appreciation

Locomotor Larry's Club (Standard 1)

Appropriate for Grades K-2

- The students use various locomotor movements to travel around the gym for two to five minutes. The students collect a clothespin at the completion of each lap and attach it to their clothing.

- When the students hear a whistle (or change of music), they switch to a different locomotor movement and continue traveling around the gym.

- The students record the number of laps on their "Locomotor Larry" form (on page 39). The number of clothespins tells them how many laps they completed.

- At the end of the week (or other time period), either place the form in the student's portfolio or send it home.

Bow WOWs!
The below adaptations address the additional standards indicated in the shaded boxes.

Standard 2: Add directionality and levels to the activity by having the students travel in specific directions or at a low, medium, or high level each time the locomotor skill is changed.

Standard 3: Have the students take Locomotor Larry home and demonstrate all eight locomotor skills for their parents/guardians.

Standard 1	Standard 2	Standard 3	Standard 4	Standard 5	Standard 6
Skills and patterns	Learning concepts	Active participation	Physical fitness	Personal/social behavior	Active appreciation

Locomotor Larry's Club

Child's Name: _____

Day One: _____ number of laps

Day Two: _____ number of laps

Day Three: _____ number of laps

Day Four: _____ number of laps

Day Five: _____ number of laps

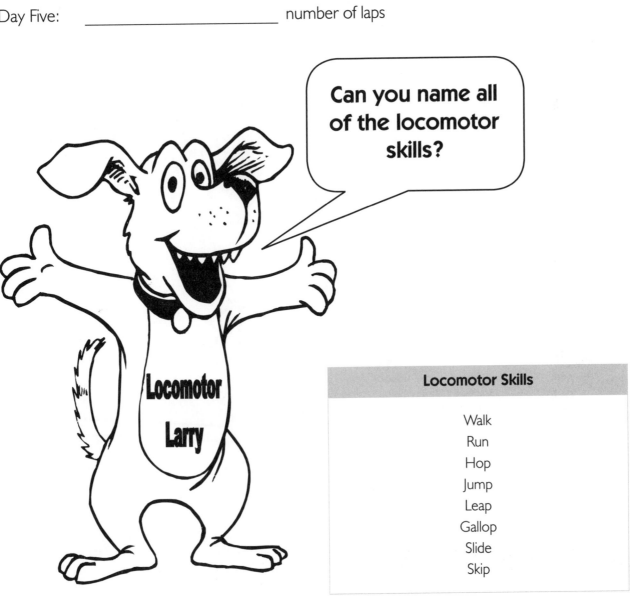

Can you name all of the locomotor skills?

Locomotor Skills
Walk
Run
Hop
Jump
Leap
Gallop
Slide
Skip

Equipment Needs
Balls or scarves

Bug Tag (Standard 1)

Appropriate for Grades K-2

- Establish boundaries for the game.

- Select two to four students to be grasshoppers. Give each grasshopper a ball (or scarf). All the other students are other types of bugs.

- Have the grasshoppers move around the playing area trying to tag the other bugs.

- If tagged, the grasshopper gives the bug the ball (or scarf) and the bug becomes a grasshopper. The grasshopper then becomes a bug.

- The new grasshopper cannot immediately tag the old grasshopper.

- To avoid being tagged, a bug may do a "Bug Jump" (i.e., tuck jump). A bug cannot be tagged while he or she is performing "Bug Jumps".

Bow WOWs!
The below adaptations address the additional standards indicated in the shaded boxes.

Standard 4: Change the activity that students have to do to avoid being tagged to tasks such as ski jumps, running in place, and jumping jacks.

Standard 1	Standard 2	Standard 3	Standard 4	Standard 5	Standard 6
Skills and patterns	Learning concepts	Active participation	Physical fitness	Personal/social behavior	Active appreciation

Beanbag Tag (Standard 1)

Equipment Needs
Beanbags, CD player, music

Appropriate for Grades 3-5

• Have each student find a partner. Each pair gets a beanbag.

• When the music starts, the students begin underhand tossing the beanbag back and forth, making good tosses to their partners.

• When the music stops, the person with the beanbag is "it." The partners begin a game of tag in which "it" walks around the activity area using the beanbag to tag his or her partner. The other partner walks quickly away to avoid being tagged.

• When tagging occurs, "it" drops the beanbag and quickly moves away from his or her partner, who has now become the tagger. The new tagger picks up the beanbag and starts quickly walking after his or her partner, This continues until the music begins again.

• When the music begins again, the partners quickly find each other and begin a new tossing and catching pattern (instead of underhand tossing).

Bow WOWs!
The below adaptations address the additional standards indicated in the shaded boxes.

Standard 5: After playing the tagging game, have the students quickly return to their partners and thank them. Give all the students five seconds to find a new partner and start the game over.

Standard 1	Standard 2	Standard 3	Standard 4	Standard 5	Standard 6
Skills and patterns	Learning concepts	Active participation	Physical fitness	Personal/social behavior	Active appreciation

Equipment Needs
None

Partner High Five (Standard 1)

Appropriate for Grades 3-5

- Organize the students into pairs and have them decide who is partner 1 and partner 2.

- Have all the 1's go to one side of the gym and all the 2's go to the opposite side. Have them line up the width of the gym.

- On a signal, each 1 chooses a locomotor skill and performs that skill as he or she moves across the gym to meet his or her partner. All of the 1's cross at the same time.

- When the 1's meet their partners on the other side of the gym, the partners exchange a high-five.

- The 2's perform that same locomotor skill (as demonstrated by their partners) back across the gym.

- When the 2's reach the other side of the gym, they do a stated/posted activity (e.g., five jumping jacks, five karate kicks, five sit-ups).

- Each 2 now chooses a different locomotor skill and starts the activity over.

Bow WOWs!
The below adaptations address the additional standards indicated in the shaded boxes.

Standard 6: In place of a locomotor skill, encourage the students to create their own movement patterns.

Standard 1	Standard 2	Standard 3	Standard 4	Standard 5	Standard 6
Skills and patterns	Learning concepts	Active participation	Physical fitness	Personal/social behavior	Active appreciation

Rubber Band Man (Standard 1)

Equipment Needs
Hoops

Appropriate for Grades 3-5

- Have each student get a hoop and hold it at waist level while standing in the middle of the hoop.

- Have the students use the hoop to bend and stretch.

- Below are some sample stretching ideas:

  o Stretch the hoop over the head.

  o Hold the hoop on the right side and bend the body to the left.

  o Move the hoop to behind the back and pull the hoop away from the body.

  o Place the hoop on the floor and place bases of support on both sides of the hoop to make a bridge.

  o Hold the hoop in one hand. See how far the other hand can stretch in the other direction.

  o While holding the hoop, use both hands to move the hoop as far to the front as possible.

  o Move the hoop slowly from above the head down to the toes.

  o Make a wide shape with the body while standing in the hoop.

Bow WOWs!
The below adaptations address the additional standards indicated in the shaded boxes.

Standard 2: Call out various movement concepts and assess whether or not the students understand the concepts and are able to create stretches using the concepts. Sample movement concepts include levels, directional motions, or differing levels of force.

Standard 5: Challenge pairs or small groups to create new stretches.

Standard 1	Standard 2	Standard 3	Standard 4	Standard 5	Standard 6
Skills and patterns	Learning concepts	Active participation	Physical fitness	Personal/social behavior	Active appreciation

Equipment Needs
Hoops, spot markers,
wall numbers

Hoops and Spots (Standard 1)

Appropriate for Grades 3-5

- In advance, place numbers on the wall. For each wall number, place a corresponding number under a spot marker.

- Scatter several different colored hoops and spot markers on the gym floor. Make sure that if there is a red spot marker that there is also a red hoop.

- Students begin at any spot marker. On a signal, the students look under their spot markers for a number. The students then run to touch the corresponding number on the wall.

- The students return to any hoop and perform 10 jumping jacks (or other appropriate activity).

- Whatever color the hoop is determines the color of the next spot marker to which the student runs. For example, if a student is in a blue hoop, then he or she moves to a blue spot marker to find the next number.

- Continue for a determined amount of time.

Bow WOWs!
The below adaptations address the additional standards indicated in the shaded boxes.

Standard 2: For older students, include a muscle name or a fitness concept with each of the wall numbers. When the students return to a hoop, they perform an activity associated with the muscle or fitness concept.

Standard 1	Standard 2	Standard 3	Standard 4	Standard 5	Standard 6
Skills and patterns	Learning concepts	Active participation	Physical fitness	Personal/social behavior	Active appreciation

Dalmatian Tag (Standard 1)

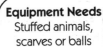

Equipment Needs
Stuffed animals,
scarves or balls

Appropriate for Grades 3-5

- Select two to four students to be taggers. Give them a tagging tail (e.g., scarf, ball).

- All of the other students carry a stuffed animal (or beanbag) around the activity area.

- The game is played like any game of tag, except, when a person is tagged, he or she must lay all collected stuffed animals at his or her feet and do 10 jumping jacks. While the tagged student is doing the jumping jacks, other players (not taggers) can steal the stuffed animals.

- Students who have had their stuffed animals stolen can steal another student's stuffed animal while he or she is doing jumping jacks.

- Play for a short amount of time and then change taggers.

Bow WOWs!
The below adaptations address the additional standards indicated in the shaded boxes.

Standard 4: After playing the game for a period of time, have the students determine their exertion level by checking their heart rates.

Standard 1	Standard 2	Standard 3	Standard 4	Standard 5	Standard 6
Skills and patterns	Learning concepts	Active participation	Physical fitness	Personal/social behavior	Active appreciation

Equipment Needs
Lummi sticks

ABC Lummi Sticks (Standard 1)

Appropriate for Grades 3-5

- From a standing position, the students say the alphabet. For each letter they say, they touch one body part with the Lummi sticks. The body parts they touch with the Lummi sticks in order are toes, knees, thighs, and shoulders.

- Have the students spell 10 words. It may help to post these words in order to reinforce the correct spelling.

- Using Lummi sticks is a great way for students to learn how to spell their spelling words. For example, when spelling the word "school," students would touch their toes with the Lummi sticks on "s," their knees on "c," their thighs on "h," their shoulders on "o," their toes on "o," and their knees on "l."

Bow WOWs!
The below adaptations address the additional standards indicated in the shaded boxes.

Standard 2: On the second day of this activity, have the students spell the words using a cross-body motion. For example, they touch their feet with uncrossed hands, cross their hands to touch their knees, touch their thighs with uncrossed hands, and cross their hands to touch their shoulders. Ask them if there was any difference in the speed of spelling with cross-body patterns.

Standard 1	Standard 2	Standard 3	Standard 4	Standard 5	Standard 6
Skills and patterns	Learning concepts	Active participation	Physical fitness	Personal/social behavior	Active appreciation

Globetrotters (Standard 1)

Equipment Needs
Balls

Appropriate for Grades 3-5

- As the students enter the gym, have each student get a ball and start running three laps while doing the activities indicated below. After finishing the laps have them go to the "ball-handling arena."

  o *First lap*: Run one lap while holding the ball. Give the teacher a high-five at the completion of the lap.

  o *Second lap*: Run the second lap while dribbling with the dominant hand. Give the teacher a high-five at the completion of the lap.

  o *Third lap*: Run the third lap dribbling with the nondominant hand. Give the teacher a high-five at the completion of the lap.

  o *Ball-handling arena*: Each day post a sign indicating what the students are to do while in the arena. Examples include 1) 10 dribbles with each hand; 2) 20 self-passes against the wall; 3) bounce the ball and spin around to catch it; and 4) five jumping jacks and 10 dribbles.

Bow WOWs!
The below adaptations address the additional standards indicated in the shaded boxes.

Standard 4: On the last lap, instead of giving the teacher a high-five have the students do 10 push-ups and 10 sit-ups.

Standard 1	Standard 2	Standard 3	Standard 4	Standard 5	Standard 6
Skills and patterns	Learning concepts	Active participation	Physical fitness	Personal/social behavior	Active appreciation

Equipment Needs
Construction paper

Happy Face Fitness (Standard 1)

Appropriate for Grades 3-5

- Make several happy faces out of different colored construction paper. Write an appropriate activity on each face (e.g., touch three walls, give 10 people a high-five, hop 10 times on each foot). In order to preserve the faces, it may help to laminate them.

- Have each student pick up a face as he or she enters class.

- When the teacher says "go," each student performs the activity stated on his or her face and then exchanges it with another student.

Bow WOWs!
The below adaptations address the additional standards indicated in the shaded boxes.

Standard 4: In order to incorporate fitness, write different types of fitness activities on the faces.

Standard 5: After this activity, give the students 20 to 30 seconds to give everyone in class a high-five and say "good morning."

Standard 1	Standard 2	Standard 3	Standard 4	Standard 5	Standard 6
Skills and patterns	Learning concepts	Active participation	Physical fitness	Personal/social behavior	Active appreciation

Double Tag (Standard 1)

Equipment Needs
Cones, pinnies

Appropriate for Grades 3-5

- Designate two different activity areas. Examples of two activity areas may be two half courts or two sides of a gym divided by cones.

- Divide the class into two groups and place each group in separate activity areas.

- Select two to four taggers per group. Give the taggers pinnies (or something similar) to identify the taggers.

- Two games of tag are played simultaneously. When a student is tagged, he or she does five jumping jacks and then joins the other game. The taggers remain in the same activity area.

- The taggers' goal is to remove all of the players from their activity area.

- Change taggers after a set amount of time.

Bow WOWs!
The below adaptations address the additional standards indicated in the shaded boxes.

Standard 4: Vary the locomotor skills after a couple of games. Add other skills to the game, such as dribbling.

Standard 1	Standard 2	Standard 3	Standard 4	Standard 5	Standard 6
Skills and patterns	Learning concepts	Active participation	Physical fitness	Personal/social behavior	Active appreciation

Equipment Needs
None

Arch Tag (Standard 1)

Appropriate for Grades 3-5

- Have each student find a partner.

- Establish the game's boundary lines.

- Identify the student who are the tagging pairs. The number of tagging pairs depends on the group size. Be sure to have enough pairs to keep the pace of the game moving quickly.

- When the game begins, the tagging pairs try to tag the other pairs. All pairs must remain connected throughout the game.

- Once a pair is tagged, the tagged pair must jog in place with their hands touching and arms raised in an arch above their heads until another pair frees them by running through the arch.

- Switch the tagging pairs often.

Bow WOWs!
The below adaptations address the additional standards indicated in the shaded boxes.

Standard 2: In the second round of the game, have each pair that goes under the arch form a four-person star with the pair they just freed by standing back-to-back with their arms spread out in front of them and touching the arms of the students next to them. This begins to add square dance concepts to the activity.

Standard 1	Standard 2	Standard 3	Standard 4	Standard 5	Standard 6
Skills and patterns	Learning concepts	Active participation	Physical fitness	Personal/social behavior	Active appreciation

Time Machine (Standard 1)

Equipment Needs
Balls, egg timers

Appropriate for Grades 3-5

- Divide students into teams of two to three players.

- Give each team a three-minute egg timer. The timers filled with sand work the best.

- Give each student a ball.

- Post a list of skills the teams can choose from to perform for the three-minute period (e.g., dribble while running laps, bounce a ball off the wall).

- Each group decides what activity to perform.

- The team turns the time machine (egg timer) over and begins the selected activity.

- When the sand runs out, the team chooses another activity and begins again.

Bow WOWs!
The below adaptations address the additional standards indicated in the shaded boxes.

Standard 4: Alternate the ball activities with fitness activities. For example, if during the first three minutes students make bounce passes to their partners, they can jog around the gym for the next three-minute period.

Standard 1	Standard 2	Standard 3	Standard 4	Standard 5	Standard 6
Skills and patterns	Learning concepts	Active participation	Physical fitness	Personal/social behavior	Active appreciation

Equipment Needs
None

Countdown to Blastoff (Standard 1)

Appropriate for Grades 3-5

- For this activity, the entire class must work together.

- The teacher has a list of 10 activities that must be completed during the countdown.

- In order to make the rocket blast off, the entire class must complete all 10 activities.

- All members of the class must complete the first activity (i.e., number 10 on the list) before the teacher says "10" (as if counting down for blast off). After all students have completed the first activity, the teacher says "10" and states the next activity.

- After all of the students complete the second activity, the teacher says "nine" and calls out the next activity. This continues until blastoff.

- On blastoff, all of the students run one lap.

- A sample countdown to blastoff list of activities is provided.

SAMPLE LIST OF ACTIVITIES

10	10 curl-ups
9	9 hops on each foot
8	8 line jumps
7	7 jumping jacks
6	6 push-ups
5	5 high-fives
4	4 pretend jump shots
3	3 mule kicks
2	run to touch 2 walls
1	1 cartwheel

BLASTOFF – Run a lap

Bow WOWs!
The below adaptations address the additional standards indicated in the shaded boxes.

Standard 4: On the second day of this activity, challenge the students to improve their time.

Standard 1	Standard 2	Standard 3	Standard 4	Standard 5	Standard 6
Skills and patterns	Learning concepts	Active participation	Physical fitness	Personal/social behavior	Active appreciation

Dirty Laundry (Standard 1)

Equipment Needs
Puzzles, clothespins

Appropriate for Grades 3-5

- Make several jigsaw puzzles, each with a different activity written on it. A sample puzzle is on the next page. Laminate the puzzle on heavy paper and cut into pieces.

- Put the puzzles in sealable plastic bags and number the bags. Place all of the bags in the center of the activity area.

- Divide the students into pairs. Each pair begins with a puzzle.

- On a signal, the pairs put their puzzles together. Upon completion of the puzzle, each pair performs the stated activity.

- When the pair completes the activity, they go and tell the teacher what was on the puzzle. The teacher then gives the pair one clothespin.

- The pair puts the first puzzle back into the bag and returns it to the center of the activity area. They then choose a different puzzle and start over.

- Continue the activity for a predetermined period of time.

- *Variation*: See how many clothespins the entire class can collect. Use this as the warm-up each day for a week. Set a goal and see if they can collect that many clothespins.

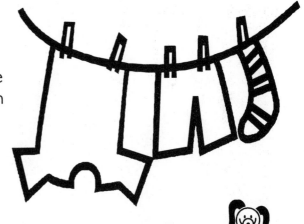

Bow WOWs!
The below adaptations address the additional standards indicated in the shaded boxes.

Standard 2: Have the students tell the teacher which health-related fitness component is associated with each of the puzzle activities.

Standard 1	Standard 2	Standard 3	Standard 4	Standard 5	Standard 6
Skills and patterns	Learning concepts	Active participation	Physical fitness	Personal/social behavior	Active appreciation

Dribble a ball 10 times

Who's the Boss? (Standard 1)

Equipment Needs
Cards

Appropriate for Grades 3-5

- Give each student one card from a deck of cards.

- Have the students begin walking throughout the activity area. Each time a student walks by another student, they have to exchange cards. This exchange phase continues for about 30 seconds.

- After about 30 seconds, the teacher calls, "Who's the boss?"

- The students quickly sort themselves into the four suits by going to designated gym corners. The student with the highest card leads the group in a fitness activity. Repeat several times.

Bow WOWs!
The below adaptations address the additional standards indicated in the shaded boxes.

Standard 2: After the students are in their correct corners, the teacher asks for a certain fitness component. The "boss" must then lead his or her group in an activity related to that fitness component.

Standard 1	Standard 2	Standard 3	Standard 4	Standard 5	Standard 6
Skills and patterns	Learning concepts	Active participation	Physical fitness	Personal/social behavior	Active appreciation

CHAPTER 3

Moo May Represent an Idea, But Only the Cow Knows It

Responsible Behaviors

All of the activities in this chapter meet Standard One (skills and patterns).
Use the "Udder Things" to meet other standards.

Helpful Hints

Responsible Behaviors

- Developing responsible and independent learners is an excellent objective. However, just because activities focus on these behaviors does not mean the students will understand what it means to be a responsible and independent learner. Never assume that the students will understand these concepts without the physical educator teaching, reinforcing, and rewarding responsible and independent behavior.

- Teach the students to teach themselves. It is impossible for teachers to spend a lot of time with every student. Students need to be taught how to act as responsible learners who can stay on task and help others in a responsible and kind manner.

- Do not assume that the planned tasks that focus on group responsibility will be enough to reach the desired outcome. The physical educator needs to tie the activity to the objective through different methods, such as teachable moments, debriefing time, and analogies.

- Give the students opportunities for leadership. Even in small groups, allow each group to have a captain who assumes an extra duty. Change leadership often.

Beat the Clock (Standard 1)

Equipment Needs
Hoops

Appropriate for Grades K-2

- Explain to the students that they only have a certain amount of time (or counts) to accomplish a specified goal.

- Practice this concept until the students understand that they must complete a task in a certain amount of time in order to "Beat the Clock."

- Below are some examples of how to practice this behavior:

  o When the teacher says "go," the students have 10 seconds to touch the wall and return to their exact spots.

  o When the teacher says "go," the students have 6 seconds to stand back-to-back with a partner.

  o When the teacher says "go," the students have 20 seconds to get a ball, bring it back, and hold it above their heads.

  o When the teacher says "go," the students have 10 seconds to form groups of three.

Udder Things
The below adaptations address the additional standards indicated in the shaded boxes.

Standard 5: Discuss with the class why it is important to beat the clock and perform the tasks quickly. In addition, discuss other ways in which the students can be responsible and complete management tasks as quickly as possible.

Standard 1	Standard 2	Standard 3	Standard 4	Standard 5	Standard 6
Skills and patterns	Learning concepts	Active participation	Physical fitness	Personal/social behavior	Active appreciation

Equipment Needs
Pictures, beanbags

General Space (Standard 1)

Appropriate for Grades K-2

- Introduce the character of General Space (whose picture is on page 61).

- Explain to the students that General Space is very happy to share his space in the gym with them, but that they must be responsible in two ways during the class.

  o The students must share the space in the gym with each other.

  o The students must move safely in the space.

- Have the students practice moving responsibly in general space. Below are some examples of how to practice this concept:

  o Each student moves from where he or she is standing to a wall without touching anyone.

  o Each student gets a beanbag and throws it in the air five different ways without bothering anyone else.

  o Each student finds a partner, holds hands, and gallops one lap around the activity area without falling down.

Udder Things
The below adaptations address the additional standards indicated in the shaded boxes.

Standard 3: Have each student take a picture of General Space home and explain the concept to his or her parents so they can practice this concept at home.

Standard 5: Have a short discussion on why it is important to share learning space/general space with the other students.

Standard 1	Standard 2	Standard 3	Standard 4	Standard 5	Standard 6
Skills and patterns	Learning concepts	Active participation	Physical fitness	Personal/social behavior	Active appreciation

Equipment Needs
Pictures

Respect and Effort (Standard 1)

Appropriate for Grades K-2

- Post pictures of Inspector Respect and Tappy Turtle on opposite walls of the gym. Their pictures are on the following two pages.

- Introduce to the students the importance of having rules by which all class members abide.

- Introduce the characters, Inspector Respect and Tappy Turtle, to the students and the rules and/or behaviors associated with each of them. Inspector Respect challenges the students to always respect themselves and others. Tappy Turtle challenges the students to always try their hardest.

- Have each student find a partner and have them decide who is partner 1 and partner 2.

- Have the partners jog one lap around the activity area and then walk over to one of the posted characters. Have partner 1 explain to partner 2 about the significance of this character.

- Have the students jog another lap and then go to the other character. This time, have partner 2 explain to partner 1 about the significance of this character.

Udder Things
The below adaptations address the additional standards indicated in the shaded boxes.

Standard 3: Have the students take pictures of both Inspector Respect and Tappy Turtle home to explain the concept to their parents.

Standard 5: Have a short discussion with the class on why it is important to respect yourself and others, and why it is important to always try your hardest.

Standard 1	Standard 2	Standard 3	Standard 4	Standard 5	Standard 6
Skills and patterns	Learning concepts	Active participation	Physical fitness	Personal/social behavior	Active appreciation

Respect Myself and Others

Inspector Respect

Try My Hardest

Tappy Turtle

Beam Me Up (Standard 1)

Equipment Needs
Hoops

Appropriate for Grades K-2

- Divide the students into pairs. Each pair needs one hoop.

- One student represents the spaceship and holds the hoop on the floor. The other student is the astronaut and stands inside the hoop.

- When the teacher calls "Beam Me Up," the student who is the spaceship raises the hoop to a level above the astronaut's head. The astronaut has now been beamed up and runs to a new spaceship.

- When the astronauts get to a new spaceship, the spaceship beams back down.

- Have the astronauts continue in this role for one minute and then switch roles with another student.

Udder Things
The below adaptations address the additional standards indicated in the shaded boxes.

Standard 3: Have the students discuss how this activity may be used at recess or during free play while at home.

Standard 5: Have a short discussion on why it is important to carefully beam up and down.

Standard 1	Standard 2	Standard 3	Standard 4	Standard 5	Standard 6
Skills and patterns	Learning concepts	Active participation	Physical fitness	Personal/social behavior	Active appreciation

Cave Dwellers (Standard 1)

Appropriate for Grades K-2

- Divide the students into pairs and have them stand on one side of the gym. Give each pair a hoop.

  - In a line in front of each pair, space five to six cones along the gym floor.

- At the starting point, each student grasps the hoop with one hand.

- On a signal, the pairs run forward to the first cone where they must stand beside the cone. One partner holds up the hoop for the other partner to crawl through. When the partner has crawled through the hoop (cave), the pair moves on to the next cone and repeats the action. This pattern continues across the gym floor until they return to the starting point.

Udder Things
The below adaptations address the additional standards indicated in the shaded boxes.

Standard 4: Add another level of fitness to this activity by having the student who did not crawl through the hoop do five jumps in and out of the hoop before they can move on to the next cone.

Standard 5: The partners discuss whether it is best for one student to crawl through all of the hoops on the way down, while the other student crawls through the hoops on the way back, or if it would be best to trade roles after each hoop.

Standard 1	Standard 2	Standard 3	Standard 4	Standard 5	Standard 6
Skills and patterns	Learning concepts	Active participation	Physical fitness	Personal/social behavior	Active appreciation

Alien Goo (Standard 1)

Equipment Needs
CD player, music

Appropriate for Grades 3-5

- Have each student find a partner.

- Have each student give a high-five with his or her right hand to his or her partner. As soon as this high-five occurs, the partners are connected as if their hands have been sprayed with alien goo. They cannot let go of each other's hands.

- While the music plays, the pair moves together throughout the activity area using locomotor skills called out by the teacher.

- When the music stops, the partners shake hands with their free hands and say "thanks for being my partner." Magically, the goo disappears and the students are free to find another partner.

- When a student finds a new partner, he or she asks, "Will you please be my partner?" As they grip hands, the alien goo returns and the new pair must now move as one.

- Repeat the activity several times.

Udder Things
The below adaptations address the additional standards indicated in the shaded boxes.

Standard 2: Have the pairs perform different tasks as the music plays. Examples are 1) do-si-do another pair, 2) form a star and spin around once, and 3) weave over and under other pairs.

Standard 1	Standard 2	Standard 3	Standard 4	Standard 5	Standard 6
Skills and patterns	Learning concepts	Active participation	Physical fitness	Personal/social behavior	Active appreciation

Equipment Needs
Balls, rubber
chickens

Spicy Hot Chicken (Standard 1)

Appropriate for Grades 3-5

- Divide the class into groups of two to three students.

- Give each student a ball and each group a rubber chicken.

- Each group member dribbles a ball with one hand while the other hand is tossing and catching the chicken among the group members.

- Count the number of catches without a miss.

- Repeat and use the nondominant hand to dribble the ball.

Udder Things
The below adaptations address the additional standards indicated in the shaded boxes.

Standard 2: Have each student in the group take a small step backward after each successful catch. Challenge each group to see how far they can move away from each other. Have the groups discuss how the throws needed to change in order to make farther throws.

Standard 5: Have the students assume responsibility for their mistakes, such as poor passes, dropping the chicken, and losing the ball.

Standard 1	Standard 2	Standard 3	Standard 4	Standard 5	Standard 6
Skills and patterns	Learning concepts	Active participation	Physical fitness	Personal/social behavior	Active appreciation

Spinning Tops (Standard 1)

Equipment Needs
Hoops

Appropriate for Grades 3-5

- Have each student get a hoop.

- Have each student stand his or her hoop up on its edge and spin it like a top.

- As the hoop begins to wobble, the student tries to jump through the hoop.

Udder Things
The below adaptations address the additional standards indicated in the shaded boxes.

Standard 2: Talk with the students about when it is best to jump through the hoop. Have them discuss how the speed of the spinning hoop affects how long it spins.

Standard 1	Standard 2	Standard 3	Standard 4	Standard 5	Standard 6
Skills and patterns	Learning concepts	Active participation	Physical fitness	Personal/social behavior	Active appreciation

Equipment Needs
Hoops, cones

Ring Roll (Standard 1)

Appropriate for Grades 3-5

- Divide the students into pairs. Each pair gets two hoops.

- Place several cones inside the target area and establish a boundary, which the students must remain behind while rolling the hoops (see illustration below).

- Partners take turns rolling the hoops in an effort to "ring" one of the cones. If they "ring" one of the cones, they claim that cone and bring it back to where they are standing.

- Continue until all of the cones have been claimed.

- *Note:* More than one area may need to be set up to accommodate the entire class. Establish what a "ring" is according to the skill level of the class.

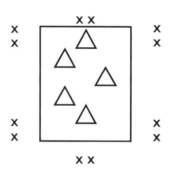

x = student

△ = cone

Udder Things

The below adaptations address the additional standards indicated in the shaded boxes.

Standard 5: After each round, stress the importance of honesty. Students need to be honest when reporting a "ring."

Standard 1	Standard 2	Standard 3	Standard 4	Standard 5	Standard 6
Skills and patterns	Learning concepts	Active participation	Physical fitness	Personal/social behavior	Active appreciation

Scram (Standard 1)

Equipment Needs
None

Appropriate for Grades 3-5

- Divide the students into groups of four. Have the groups line up in a single-file line at a designated starting point. Have the students put their hands on the shoulders of the person in front of them.

- On a signal, each group takes three steps forward.

- As soon as the third step is taken, the first person in the line runs around his or her group three times.

- After the third time around the group, he or she goes to the back of the line and the group takes another three steps forward. The new person at the front of the line runs around the group three times.

- This process continues until the teams cross the designated area.

Udder Things
The below adaptations address the additional standards indicated in the shaded boxes.

Standard 2 and 5: After each trip across the designated area, the students should give each other a high-five and plan a strategy to improve their time for the next round.

Standard 1	Standard 2	Standard 3	Standard 4	Standard 5	Standard 6
Skills and patterns	Learning concepts	Active participation	Physical fitness	Personal/social behavior	Active appreciation

Equipment Needs
None

Alphabet Groups (Standard 1)

Appropriate for Grades 3-5

• Divide the class into groups of five.

• One person in each group is designated as the leader. The other group members lie down on the floor.

• On a signal, the four group members try to form the letter "A," while lying on the floor.

• When the leader sees the letter "A," he or she says the letter out loud. The group then tries to create the letter "B," and so on.

• When the group reaches the letter "G," the leader changes. Change leaders at the letters "G," "K," "P," and "U."

• The object is to be the first group to make all the letters of the alphabet.

Udder Things
The below adaptations address the additional standards indicated in the shaded boxes.

Standard 5: The leader should not only call out the next letter, but he or she should also act as a motivational leader to motivate the group to form the letters as quickly as possible.

Standard 1	Standard 2	Standard 3	Standard 4	Standard 5	Standard 6
Skills and patterns	Learning concepts	Active participation	Physical fitness	Personal/social behavior	Active appreciation

"When You Have Got an Elephant by the Hind Leg, and He Is Trying to Run Away, It's Best to Let Him Run"

—Abraham Lincoln

Locomotor Skills

All of the activities in this chapter meet Standard One (skills and patterns).
Use the "Forget Me Nots" to meet other standards.

Helpful Hints

Locomotor Skills

- To assist in the teaching of the various locomotor skills, use the cues offered in Chapter 1.

- Incorporation of locomotor skills into fitness activities, rhythms, and various games is fairly easy to accomplish and highly encouraged.

- The eight most common locomotor skills are walking, running, jumping, hopping, leaping, galloping, sliding, and skipping. Some physical educators have other creative names for some of the locomotors skills. Below are some examples:

    o *Lump:* This is a leap (i.e., taking off from one foot) that lands on two feet.

    o *Jeep:* This is a jump (i.e., taking off from both feet) that lands on one foot.

    o *Humpty Dumpty:* This is two hops on the left foot, followed by two hops on the right foot.

Astronauts (Standard 1)

Equipment Needs
Hoops

Appropriate for Grades K-2

- Have each student get a hoop and place it on the floor. This is each student's individual spaceship. Tell the students to get into their spaceships by stepping into the middle of the hoops.

- Have the students take off from the spaceship by jumping out of the hoop.

- Once the students are outside their hoops, tell them to run and touch a specific object (e.g., walls, bleachers, ball cart).

- On their run back to the spaceship, have them jump and land inside the spaceship.

Forget Me Nots
The below adaptations address the additional standards indicated in the shaded boxes.

Standard 2: Have the students determine various methods of traveling. Ask them to change speed, direction, and/or level.

Standard 4: After the students know the sequence of the activity, increase the intensity by having them do a countdown by jumping in place ten times before leaving the spaceship. When they return to their spaceships, have them quickly jog in place inside the hoop until the teacher calls "Power Down." At that time, give the students five seconds to find a new spaceship before starting a new sequence.

Standard 1	Standard 2	Standard 3	Standard 4	Standard 5	Standard 6
Skills and patterns	Learning concepts	Active participation	Physical fitness	Personal/social behavior	Active appreciation

Equipment Needs
Jump ropes

River Jumping (Standard 1)

Appropriate for Grades K-2

- Each student stretches a jump rope on the floor and practices jumping over the rope several times.

- Have each student find a partner.

- The partners place their two jump ropes on the floor about six inches apart and take turns trying to jump the ropes (i.e., the river).

- As they get better, encourage them to move the ropes farther apart.

- Once they have mastered this task, have the pairs place their jump ropes back in their original positions of about six inches apart.

- Have the students stand in the river (i.e., the area between the ropes) and attempt to jump to the shores (i.e., the area outside the ropes.)

- As they get better, encourage them to increase the size of the river.

Forget Me Nots
The below adaptations address the additional standards indicated in the shaded boxes.

Standard 4: To add difficulty to the jumping, have the students place their hands on the shores and their feet in the river and then jump so that their feet land on the same shore as their hands. In addition, to raise their heart rates, have the students jump the river continuously for 30 seconds. Have them determine their heart rates at the end of the time period.

Standard 1	Standard 2	Standard 3	Standard 4	Standard 5	Standard 6
Skills and patterns	Learning concepts	Active participation	Physical fitness	Personal/social behavior	Active appreciation

Fire Engine (Standard 1)

Equipment Needs
Cones

Appropriate for Grades K-2

- Establish boundaries for the activity area.

- Have each student get a cone and place it in the activity area.

- When the teacher calls, "Go fire engines," the students jog (or another locomotor skill) among the cones.

- When the teacher calls, "Put the fire out," each student quickly returns to his or her original cone, picks up the cone, sets it back down on the floor, and says, "Fire's out."

- Repeat the activity using different locomotor skills.

Forget Me Nots
The below adaptations address the additional standards indicated in the shaded boxes.

Standard 4: Begin to add other task options to allow for the continuation of the activity. Some examples are below:

a) When the teacher calls, "Slide down the pole," the students lie on the floor beside their cones and perform sit-ups.

b) When the teacher calls "Emergency," the students must run and touch at least three walls before returning to their cones.

c) When the teacher calls "Danger," the students must move at a low level with a partner.

Standard 1	Standard 2	Standard 3	Standard 4	Standard 5	Standard 6
Skills and patterns	Learning concepts	Active participation	Physical fitness	Personal/social behavior	Active appreciation

Equipment Needs
Paper plates,
animal pictures,
CD player, music

Animal Crackers (Standard 1)

Appropriate for Grades K-2

- Tape pictures of animals to paper plates.
  Sample pictures are provided on page 79.

- Spread the plates out face down in the center of the activity area.

- When the music begins, the students jog (or another locomotor skill) around the outside of the activity area.

- When the music stops, each student quickly finds a plate to stand by.

- After the teacher instructs the students to turn their plates over, have the students identify the animal on their plates and move like that animal.

- When the music begins again, the students start to perform another locomotor skill around the outside of the activity area.

Forget Me Nots
The below adaptations address the additional standards indicated in the shaded boxes.

Standard 2: Have the students make the first letter of the animal's name with their bodies.

Standard 4: After playing the game for a few rounds, have the students perform a specific task (e.g., balance, jumps, hops) for a specific number of times before turning the plate over.

Standard 1	Standard 2	Standard 3	Standard 4	Standard 5	Standard 6
Skills and patterns	Learning concepts	Active participation	Physical fitness	Personal/social behavior	Active appreciation

Equipment Needs
Hoops

Tater Tot Trot (Standard 1)

Appropriate for Grades K-2

- Have each student find a partner. Each pair gets one hoop.

- One partner steps into the hoop, brings the hoop to his or her waist, and holds the hoop in that position. This student is the tater tot in a frying pan.

- The other partner stands behind his or her partner on the outside of the hoop and holds onto the hoop. This partner is the cooker.

- Have the pairs gallop one lap around the activity area. The partners then exchange places and gallop a second lap.

Forget Me Nots
The below adaptations address the additional standards indicated in the shaded boxes.

Standard 5: Make sure the pair is moving at a safe speed for both partners. Have them tell each other at the end of each lap whether or not the speed was appropriate. Have them thank each other for being respectful.

Standard 1	Standard 2	Standard 3	Standard 4	Standard 5	Standard 6
Skills and patterns	Learning concepts	Active participation	Physical fitness	Personal/social behavior	Active appreciation

Puddle Jumping (Standard 1)

Equipment Needs
Spot markers, lummi sticks

Appropriate for Grades K-2

- Have the students place spot markers in a large circle around the activity area. It is a good idea to add a few extra spot markers to the circle in order to allow for safe spacing of the students.

- Each student stands on a spot marker and faces counterclockwise. The students then jump from one spot marker (puddle) to the next until they return to their original puddle.

- In the second round, the students jump from their starting spot markers and land straddling the next spot marker. The students then step back onto the new spot marker with both feet before jumping to straddle the next spot marker. They continue this until they return to their original puddles.

- In the third round, the students jump from one spot marker to the next. The teacher holds a lummi stick horizontally, slightly off the floor, between two of the spot markers in the circle. When the students reach the spot marker before the lummi stick, they must jump up and over the stick in order to get to the other spot marker. This continues until all of the students have had a chance to jump the lummi sticks.

- In the last round, half of the students hold a lummi stick between various spot markers. When a student comes to a lummi stick, he or she must jump up and over the stick. Repeat for the second half of the students.

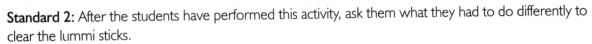

Forget Me Nots
The below adaptations address the additional standards indicated in the shaded boxes.

Standard 2: After the students have performed this activity, ask them what they had to do differently to clear the lummi sticks.

Standard 4: To increase their heart rate levels, have the students perform several laps around the spot markers (e.g., jump a lap, leap a lap, straddle jump a lap, run a lap around the outside of the spots, skip a lap inside the spots). Be sure to assess each student's heart rate after the final lap.

Standard 1	Standard 2	Standard 3	Standard 4	Standard 5	Standard 6
Skills and patterns	Learning concepts	Active participation	Physical fitness	Personal/social behavior	Active appreciation

Equipment Needs
Spot markers

Checkers (Standard 1)

Appropriate for Grades K-2

- Have the students place numerous spot markers of different colors around the activity area.

- The teacher calls out a locomotor skill that students must perform in order to move to specific spots. Below are some examples of what the teacher might call out:

  o Hop on the right foot to a red spot.

  o Jump to a blue spot.

  o Slide to a green spot.

  o Walk backward to a yellow spot.

  o Gallop to a blue spot.

  o Jump sideways to a yellow spot.

  o Hop on the left foot to a blue spot.

  o Jump to a red spot and then walk around it.

  o Slide to a green spot and make a shape with the body.

Forget Me Nots
The below adaptations address the additional standards indicated in the shaded boxes.

Standard 5: After playing the game several times, have the students find partners. Instruct the partners to work together to move from spot to spot. Below are some examples of partner motions:

1. With backs touching, slide to a red spot.

2. While giving high-fives, jump to a green spot.

3. With elbows hooked, skip to a yellow spot.

After two or three motions, have the students thank their current partners and quickly find a different partner.

Standard 1	Standard 2	Standard 3	Standard 4	Standard 5	Standard 6
Skills and patterns	Learning concepts	Active participation	Physical fitness	Personal/social behavior	Active appreciation

Bus Stop (Standard 1)

Equipment Needs
Spot markers, cones

Appropriate for Grades K-2

- Each student gets a spot marker and a cone. The equipment should be set up on the floor as illustrated below.

- Each student starts on his or her spot (bus) on the floor.

- The cone (bus stop) is placed at a distance (determined by the teacher) behind each student.

- The teacher calls out locomotor skill and then calls "Bus Stop."

- The students perform the locomotor skill to the cone and back.

Center Line

Forget Me Nots
The below adaptations address the additional standards indicated in the shaded boxes.

Standard 2: After playing the game several times, have the students do peer-assessments. Have students on one side of the gym do the locomotor skill to the "bus stop" and back, while the other students stay at the center line and do the assessment. Remember to give the assessors criteria for the skill to be checked.

Standard 4: Add various fitness activities either at the cone or at the bus stop.

Standard 1	Standard 2	Standard 3	Standard 4	Standard 5	Standard 6
Skills and patterns	Learning concepts	Active participation	Physical fitness	Personal/social behavior	Active appreciation

Equipment Needs
Jump ropes

Climbing the Mountain (Standard 1)

Appropriate for Grades K-2

- Have the students get into groups of three. Each group gets one jump rope.

- Two students in the group hold the rope about six inches off the ground.

- The third student jumps over the jump rope and then moves to the next group's rope to jump. The student jumps each group's rope until he or she returns to his or her original group.

- Each jumper trades positions with one of the jump rope holders in his or her group.

- Continue until all three members of the group (and each student in the class) have completed the activity.

- After all the students have performed this skill, start the activity again, but have the jump rope holders sway the rope back and forth. Instruct the students to jump when the rope is coming toward them.

Forget Me Nots
The below adaptations address the additional standards indicated in the shaded boxes.

Standard 5: Talk to the students about how important it is to respect others and not raise the rope too high or swing the rope too fast.

Standard 1	Standard 2	Standard 3	Standard 4	Standard 5	Standard 6
Skills and patterns	Learning concepts	Active participation	Physical fitness	Personal/social behavior	Active appreciation

Locomotor Relay (Standard 1)

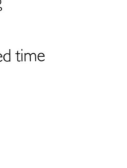

Equipment Needs
None

Appropriate for Grades 3-5

- Have each student find a partner.

- Designate a line on the floor from which the students will start.

- In relay style, the partners take turns moving across the activity area using the locomotor skill stated by the teacher.

- Have the partners count the number of trips they make during the allotted time (e.g., 90 seconds).

- Change the locomotor skill and begin the next relay.

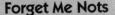

Forget Me Nots
The below adaptations address the additional standards indicated in the shaded boxes.

Standard 2: Have the partners count their trips by twos or threes. If appropriate, have them count their trips in another language.

Standard 5: Have each pair challenge another pair. After the allotted time, have the pairs tell each other how many trips they made. Have the pair that made the least amount of trips congratulate the other pair and have the pair that made the most trips thank the other pair for playing.

Standard 1	Standard 2	Standard 3	Standard 4	Standard 5	Standard 6
Skills and patterns	Learning concepts	Active participation	Physical fitness	Personal/social behavior	Active appreciation

Equipment Needs
None

Leaping Lizards (Standard 1)

Appropriate for Grades 3-5

- Have each student find a partner.

- One of the partners performs a leap. The other partner mimics the same leap.

- Change the leader and repeat.

- After a short amount of time, have the students find new partners.

Forget Me Nots
The below adaptations address the additional standards indicated in the shaded boxes.

Standard 6: Give the students a descriptor that they must perform in their leaps. Some examples might include 1) adding a clap; 2) leaping and turn; 3) leaping at a low level; or 4) adding a piece of equipment. Allow them to create a leaping pattern.

Standard 1	Standard 2	Standard 3	Standard 4	Standard 5	Standard 6
Skills and patterns	Learning concepts	Active participation	Physical fitness	Personal/social behavior	Active appreciation

Save the Puppies (Standard 1)

Equipment Needs
Spot Markers, stuffed animals or beanbags

Appropriate for Grades 3-5

- Scatter many spot markers throughout the gym.

- Scatter numerous stuffed animals or beanbags (puppies) at one end of the gym.

- Divide the students into pairs.

- The pairs start on the opposite side of the gym from the stuffed animals.

- To begin the activity, the first partner starts jumping from spot marker to spot marker across the gym. When this partner gets to the other side of the gym, the student gets a "puppy" and crosses back over the spot markers to his or her partner.

- The second partner now crosses the gym (again using only the spot markers) to save a second puppy.

- Continue the game until all of the puppies have been collected.

- Begin a new game using a hop or leap instead of a jump when crossing the area with spot markers.

Forget Me Nots
The below adaptations address the additional standards indicated in the shaded boxes.

Standard 2: After playing this game one time, allow the students 15 seconds to reposition any spot marker they think would allow for a better crossing pattern.

Standard 4: More "puppies" allow the game to last much longer. Play this game two to three times to increase the heart rate levels for a longer period of time. Be sure to assess each student's heart rate after the final game.

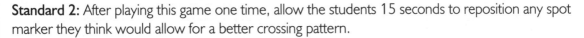

Standard 1	Standard 2	Standard 3	Standard 4	Standard 5	Standard 6
Skills and patterns	Learning concepts	Active participation	Physical fitness	Personal/social behavior	Active appreciation

Equipment Needs
Cones, spot markers, dice

Roller Derby (Standard 1)

Appropriate for Grades 3-5

- Create a large circle of cones or spot markers. Have the students stand inside the circle.

- The teacher rolls the dice. The number on the dice indicates the number of cones or spot markers the students must travel completely around before returning to the center of the circle.

- The teacher may call out any locomotor skill to be used to travel around the cones or spot markers. For example, if the dice reads "three," the teacher may say, "Skip around three spot markers." The students would then skip completely around three spot markers before returning to the center.

- In addition, the teacher may call a color. For example, if the dice shows "five," the teacher may say, "Gallop around five different blue cones and spot markers." The students would then gallop around five different blue cones and five different blue spot markers before returning to the center.

Forget Me Nots
The below adaptations address the additional standards indicated in the shaded boxes.

Standard 2: Allow the students to add rules they think would be appropriate for the game. For example, they have to give at least two people a high-five while they are traveling.

Standard 5: After playing the game several times, introduce diversity through the directions stated. Some examples are 1) different ages go to different colored cones; 2) boys go to one color and girls go to a different color; and 3) students with brothers go to one color and students without brothers go to a different color.

Standard 1	Standard 2	Standard 3	Standard 4	Standard 5	Standard 6
Skills and patterns	Learning concepts	Active participation	Physical fitness	Personal/social behavior	Active appreciation

Traffic Jam (Standard 1)

Equipment Needs
Spot Markers

Appropriate for Grades 3-5

- Place several spot markers on the gym floor.

- The students move throughout the activity area doing selected locomotor activities.

- The teacher calls various traffic commands. Some sample commands are below:

    o School zone—walking

    o Bumpy road—skipping

    o Narrow road—galloping

    o Road construction—leaping over the potholes (spot markers)

    o Flat tire—hopping on one leg

    o Interstate driving—running

    o Out of gas—take a break and sit down

    o Traffic jam—get in groups of three, put hands on the shoulders of the person in front, and walk

    o Rain on the road—jumping jacks (windshield wipers)

    o Emergency—freeze

    o Ambulance—move to edges of the gym

    o Stuck in the mud—jog in place

    o Icy road—sliding (skating)

    o Detour—walking backward

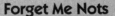

Forget Me Nots
The below adaptations address the additional standards indicated in the shaded boxes.

Standard 2: Have each student find a partner and challenge them with the traffic commands. This will reinforce these concepts.

Standard 1	Standard 2	Standard 3	Standard 4	Standard 5	Standard 6
Skills and patterns	Learning concepts	Active participation	Physical fitness	Personal/social behavior	Active appreciation

Equipment Needs
Colored tape

Air Bud (Standard 1)

Appropriate for Grades 3-5

- Make three to five marks at increasing heights (one above the other) at various points on the gym walls using different colored tape.

- Have the students run a lap in which they stop at each point along the gym walls to jump and touch the highest mark they can.

- Be sure to have some marks low enough where all students can reach them, as well as some marks that will challenge even the most athletic students.

Forget Me Nots
The below adaptations address the additional standards indicated in the shaded boxes.

Standard 2: Have the students discuss what techniques they are using to jump higher (e.g., one foot, two foot, approach, no approach). In addition, have the students assess a partner's jump. The assessors should be looking for such things as arms initiating the jump, body extension, and hands above the head.

Standard 1	Standard 2	Standard 3	Standard 4	Standard 5	Standard 6
Skills and patterns	Learning concepts	Active participation	Physical fitness	Personal/social behavior	Active appreciation

Huff and Puff (Standard 1)

Equipment Needs
Spot Markers, cards

Appropriate for Grades 3-5

- Place several spot markers on the floor in the designated activity area. Attach cards with a number (up to 15) and a locomotor skill (e.g., three leaps or seven jumps) on the underside of each spot marker.

- Post the numbers 1 through 15 on the walls.

- Have each student start on a spot marker. The student looks under the spot marker to determine the number and the locomotor skill to be performed.

- After completing the skill, the student runs to tag the number posted on the wall that corresponds with the number of repetitions just completed.

- The student then returns to the activity area and goes to any vacant spot marker. Challenge the students to complete as many spots as possible in a certain period of time.

Forget Me Nots
The below adaptations address the additional standards indicated in the shaded boxes.

Standard 4: To increase the heart rate levels, when the students approach the number posted on the wall, have them perform the same number of jumping jacks (or other fitness activity) as the number posted. Be sure to assess heart rate after an appropriate amount of time.

Standard 5: After the students have participated in the activity, have the students find partners and repeat the activity. This time instruct them to multiply the number on each card by two and complete that many of the designated locomotor skill before running to the posted number on the wall.

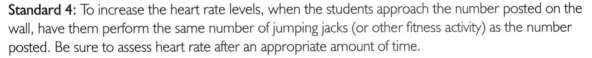

Standard 1	Standard 2	Standard 3	Standard 4	Standard 5	Standard 6
Skills and patterns	Learning concepts	Active participation	Physical fitness	Personal/social behavior	Active appreciation

CHAPTER 5

If You Dance with a Bear, You'd Better Let Him Lead

Throwing, Catching, Kicking, and Dribbling

All of the activities in this chapter meet Standard One (skills and patterns). Use the "GRR-reat Ideas" to meet other standards.

Helpful Hints

Throwing, Catching, Kicking, and Dribbling

- When teaching basic sport skills, it is always best to have a ball, hoop, racket, or other piece of equipment available for each student. If this is not possible, the next best thing is to have a ball, hoop, racket, or other piece of equipment available for every two students. The students cannot work on improving their skills unless they have a lot of practice with the necessary equipment.

- To encourage maximum participation, never have a relay team with more than three people.

- It is perfectly appropriate to change the court or field boundaries. Using smaller activity spaces allows teams to have fewer students on them. Do not worry about using regulation nets; using a rope as a net is sufficient.

- The fewer students on a team, the more skill repetitions the students receive.

- Official equipment is not absolutely necessary. Put out more equipment for the class and use equipment that fits the skill level of the students. For elementary school students, light and/or trainer balls are better than regulation balls.

Pepper Pops (Standard 1)

Equipment Needs
Hoops, striking objects, CD player, music

Appropriate for Grades K-2

- Have the students stand beside a hoop in which several striking objects have been placed. Striking objects might include balloons, scarves, sponge balls, feather balls, beanbags, etc.

- When the music begins to play, each student gets an object out of a hoop and begins striking that object with his or her hand.

- When the music stops, the students return their objects to the hoop and retrieve a different striking object.

- Repeat this activity several times.

GRR-reat Ideas
The below adaptations address the additional standards indicated in the shaded boxes.

Standard 2: Have each student discuss with a partner which objects were the easiest and the hardest to strike.

Standard 6: Have each student find a partner. Allow the pairs to choose their favorite item for striking and create a striking pattern. After an allotted time period, have the partners show another pair their pattern. Partners who are watching should applaud after the demonstration.

Standard 1	Standard 2	Standard 3	Standard 4	Standard 5	Standard 6
Skills and patterns	Learning concepts	Active participation	Physical fitness	Personal/social behavior	Active appreciation

Equipment Needs
Scarves

Scarf Sequence (Standard 1)

Appropriate for Grades K-2

- Have the students toss a scarf to themselves and catch it at a high level, then at a medium level, and finally at a low level. Repeat three times.

- Have the students toss their scarves under their right legs and catch them. Then toss them under their left legs and catch them. Repeat three times.

- Have the students toss and catch their scarves on three different body parts.

- Repeat the above in a movement sequence.

GRR-reat Ideas
The below adaptations address the additional standards indicated in the shaded boxes.

Standard 2: Use this activity as a quick assessment for knowledge of the various levels.

Standard 6: Have the students create their own toss-and-catch patterns. After an allotted time period, have half of the class show the other half of the class their patterns. Students who are watching should applaud after the demonstration, and then allow the other half to demonstrate their patterns.

Standard 1	Standard 2	Standard 3	Standard 4	Standard 5	Standard 6
Skills and patterns	Learning concepts	Active participation	Physical fitness	Personal/social behavior	Active appreciation

Balloon Toss (Standard 1)

Equipment Needs
Balloons

Appropriate for Grades K-2

- Have each student toss and catch a balloon in a variety of ways. Remind the students to keep their eyes on their balloons.

- Below are some examples of tosses and catches:

    o See how many throws it takes to move the balloon across the gym.

    o Toss the balloon up and catch it with both hands.

    o Toss the balloon as high as possible and catch it.

    o Toss the balloon up and catch it on the elbow.

    o Toss the balloon up and touch the knees (or ankles, shoulders, hips) before catching the balloon.

    o Toss the balloon up and turn around before catching it.

    o Toss the balloon up with one hand and catch it with the other hand.

    o Toss the balloon up and catch it on the back.

    o Toss the balloon up and lie down to catch it.

    o Toss the balloon up and catch it as low as possible.

GRR-reat Ideas
The below adaptations address the additional standards indicated in the shaded boxes.

Standard 6: Have the students create a new toss-and-catch pattern. Allow each student to demonstrate it for a partner. Have the partners put their two patterns together to make a longer pattern.

Standard 1	Standard 2	Standard 3	Standard 4	Standard 5	Standard 6
Skills and patterns	Learning concepts	Active participation	Physical fitness	Personal/social behavior	Active appreciation

Equipment Needs
Small lasso ropes, hoops, spot markers, cones

Lasso Throws (Standard 1)

Appropriate for Grades K-2

- Cut soft rope (e.g., soft clothesline rope) into 10- to 12-inch strips. Tie the ends of each strip together to make a loop. These are the lassos.

- Have each student find a partner.

- Using the underhand toss, have the students practice throwing lassos in several different ways.

- Below are some ideas for throwing:

  o See how many throws it takes to move the lasso across the gym.

  o Toss the lasso back and forth with a partner.

  o Standing on a line, throw the lasso into a hoop that is lying on the floor.

  o Standing on a line, throw the lasso so that it lands around a spot marker.

  o Standing on a line, throw the lasso over a pony (cone).

GRR-reat Ideas
The below adaptations address the additional standards indicated in the shaded boxes.

Standard 2: Have the students discuss the best ways to throw the lasso in order to achieve the desired goal.

Standard 5: Have the students toss the lasso back and forth with a partner. Encourage them to thank their partner after 10 throws and then move on to find a new partner.

Standard 1	Standard 2	Standard 3	Standard 4	Standard 5	Standard 6
Skills and patterns	Learning concepts	Active participation	Physical fitness	Personal/social behavior	Active appreciation

Roll and Throw (Standard 1)

Equipment Needs
Beanbags, cones, dice

Appropriate for Grades K-2

- Have each student find a partner.

- Each pair gets a beanbag, a die, and a cone. The pairs place the cone on a line on the opposite side of the activity area.

- The first partner rolls the die and takes that many steps toward the cone before throwing the beanbag at the cone. The type of throw may be specified by the teacher or the students may decide which throw would be best to use depending on the distance they are from the target.

- The first partner retrieves his or her beanbag and returns to the starting point. The second partner now rolls the die and takes that many steps toward the cone and throws the beanbag at the cone. The second partner retrieves his or her beanbag and returns to the starting point.

- Have the students repeat this activity several times.

GRR-reat Ideas
The below adaptations address the additional standards indicated in the shaded boxes.

Standard 2: After a short time, discuss how it may be better to use an underhand throw when the distance is shorter, while an overhand throw may be better when the distance is longer.

Standard 5: Have the partners thank each other and then find a new partner to play a new round.

Standard 1	Standard 2	Standard 3	Standard 4	Standard 5	Standard 6
Skills and patterns	Learning concepts	Active participation	Physical fitness	Personal/social behavior	Active appreciation

Equipment Needs
Spot markers,
bouncing balls

101 Dalmatians (Standard 1)

Appropriate for Grades 3-5

- Scatter several spot markers throughout the playing area.

- Each student gets a ball and must dribble 10 times on 10 different spot markers (100 times).

- When a student finishes 100 dribbles, he or she goes to the teacher, dribbles one time in front of the teacher (101!!), and gives the teacher a high-five.

- As soon as the students finish, they go to the ball-handling arena until the other students complete the skill.

- Post a sign in the ball-handling arena that indicates what the students do in the arena. Examples include 1) 10 dribbles with each hand; 2) self-pass 20 times against the wall; 3) bounce the ball and turn around to catch it 10 times; and 4) 5 jumping jacks then 10 dribbles.

GRR-reat Ideas
The below adaptations address the additional standards indicated in the shaded boxes.

Standard 2: Discuss with the students how the height of the dribble affects the speed of the dribble (e.g., the lower the dribble, the faster the dribble).

Standard 3: Make balls available during recess and before and after school in order to encourage the students to practice their dribbling skills.

Standard 5: Have the students complete the entire activity with a partner. Have each student attempt to dribble the ball at the same speed as his or her partner.

Standard 1	Standard 2	Standard 3	Standard 4	Standard 5	Standard 6
Skills and patterns	Learning concepts	Active participation	Physical fitness	Personal/social behavior	Active appreciation

Chipmunks (Standard 1)

Equipment Needs
Bounce balls, plastic cups, poker chips

Appropriate for Grades 3-5

- Have each student get a ball that bounces.

- Place 8 to 10 plastic cups around the gym. Spread out a large number of poker chips (i.e., three or four times the number of students) on the gym floor.

- Each student dribbles his or her ball around the gym and tries to pick up poker chips and put them in a cup. Each student must continually dribble while doing this task.

- This process continues until all of the poker chips have been placed into the cups.

GRR-reat Ideas
The below adaptations address the additional standards indicated in the shaded boxes.

Standard 5: Do a timed round (e.g., two minutes) and see how many poker chips the class can get into the cups. For the next timed round, have the class set a goal for how many they can get in the cup.

Standard 1	Standard 2	Standard 3	Standard 4	Standard 5	Standard 6
Skills and patterns	Learning concepts	Active participation	Physical fitness	Personal/social behavior	Active appreciation

Equipment Needs
Balls

Snow Blower (Standard 1)

Appropriate for Grades 3-5

- Divide the students into groups of four. Each group gets one ball.

- One student in each group is the snow blower. He or she stands with the ball in front of the other three group members (see illustration below).

- The snow blower tosses the ball to the first team member who then passes the ball back to the snow blower. The snow blower then passes the ball to the second player and third player.

- When the third player throws the ball back to the snow blower, the snow blower passes the ball back to the third player, then the second player, and finally the first player.

- Continue this activityfor one minute and then change snow blowers and the type of pass used.

Player 1	**Player 2**	**Player 3**
	Snow Blower	

GRR-reat Ideas
The below adaptations address the additional standards indicated in the shaded boxes.

Standard 4: Before changing snow blowers, the snow blower must lead a cardiovascular activity for 30 seconds.

Standard 1	Standard 2	Standard 3	Standard 4	Standard 5	Standard 6
Skills and patterns	Learning concepts	Active participation	Physical fitness	Personal/social behavior	Active appreciation

555 (Standard 1)

Equipment Needs
Throwing objects

Appropriate for Grades 3-5

• *Throwing 555*: Have each student design with a partner a throwing pattern that demonstrates five underhand throws, five overhand throws, and five throws at a target. Repeat with a different throwing object.

• *Catching 555*: Have each student design with a partner a throwing pattern that demonstrates how to throw and catch five different-sized objects (i.e., playground ball, football, yarn ball, rubber chicken, Frisbee). Have the pairs demonstrate different ways to catch the objects.

GRR-reat Ideas
The below adaptations address the additional standards indicated in the shaded boxes.

Standard 2: After completing this activity several times, have the students add other movement concepts to the throwing and catching pattern. For example, they could add rhythm, pathways, connections, speed, or force.

Standard 6: Have the pairs demonstrate their pattern to another pair.

Standard 1	Standard 2	Standard 3	Standard 4	Standard 5	Standard 6
Skills and patterns	Learning concepts	Active participation	Physical fitness	Personal/social behavior	Active appreciation

Luck of the Draw (Standard 1)

Appropriate for Grades 3-5

• Divide the class into groups of two to three students and give each group a deck of cards. Have the groups find a spot in general space.

• The groups lay their cards on the floor in their space.

• One person from each group turns over the first card. The group members look at the reference chart to see which ball they have to use and how many tosses they have to make.

• The number on the card is the number of times the team tosses the object before turning over another card. If a face card is drawn, the group must complete 15 tosses, Aces are worth 20 tosses, and Jokers are worth 25 tosses. The suit on the card determines what object the group has to toss: Spades = tennis ball, Hearts = beanbags, Clubs = spider balls, Diamonds = playground balls, and Jokers = rubber chickens.

Luck of the Draw Reference Chart

Numbered cards = # tosses
Face Cards = 15 tosses
Aces = 20 tosses
Jokers = 25 tosses

Spades = Tennis balls
(Sit-ups)

Hearts = Beanbags
(Running in place)

Clubs = Spider balls
(Mountain climbers)

Diamonds = Playground balls
(Ski jumps)

Jokers = Rubber chickens
(Push-ups)

GRR-reat Ideas
The below adaptations address the additional standards indicated in the shaded boxes.

Standard 4: For each card, develop a fitness activity. Students toss the objects and then perform the fitness activity for that number of times. The fitness activities are listed in the reference chart and determined by the suit of the card.

Standard 1	Standard 2	Standard 3	Standard 4	Standard 5	Standard 6
Skills and patterns	Learning concepts	Active participation	Physical fitness	Personal/social behavior	Active appreciation

Sheep Dogs (Standard 1)

Equipment Needs
Balloons, tokens
(e.g., clothespins)

Appropriate for Grades 3-5

- Establish boundries for the activity area.

- Choose three to five students to be sheep dogs. These students try to catch the sheep (balloons) that are being hit across the activity area.

- Give each of the other students a balloon. These students try to tap their sheep (balloons) across the activity area without being captured by the sheep dogs.

- In order for a sheep dog to capture a sheep, the sheep dog must catch the balloon. If a sheep is captured, the sheep dog hands the sheep back to its owner, who must now return to the starting line and try to cross the activity area again.

- If a student makes it across the activity area with his or her sheep, he or she gets a token (e.g., a clothespin) for being successful.

- After receiving a token, the student runs back across the area to the starting line to try crossing again.

GRR-reat Ideas
The below adaptations address the additional standards indicated in the shaded boxes.

Standard 4: Before or after playing Sheep Dogs, allow the students to have "sheep" races across the area. The students strike the balloons across the activity area without the sheep dogs trying to prevent them from crossing. Students can challenge other students in the class if they wish.

Standard 1	Standard 2	Standard 3	Standard 4	Standard 5	Standard 6
Skills and patterns	Learning concepts	Active participation	Physical fitness	Personal/social behavior	Active appreciation

Equipment Needs
Fling its or stuffed animals

Fling Its (Standard 1)

Appropriate for Grades 3-5

- Have each student find a partner. Give each pair a fling it or a stuffed animal.

- Using the fling its (or stuffed animals), the pairs can perform some of the following skill development ideas:

    o The pairs toss and catch the stuffed animal.

    o The partners toss and catch the stuffed animal, but attempt to touch right hands together before each catch.

    o The partners toss, "wring the dishrag," and catch the stuffed animal.

    o The partners toss and catch two different stuffed animals.

    o The partners toss and catch the stuffed animal, and try to get it to flip over while in the air.

GRR-reat Ideas
The below adaptations address the additional standards indicated in the shaded boxes.

Standard 6: Have the pairs invent a trick using the fling its. Have each pair share their trick with other pairs. Allow practice time so that the students can try each other's creations.

Standard 1	Standard 2	Standard 3	Standard 4	Standard 5	Standard 6
Skills and patterns	Learning concepts	Active participation	Physical fitness	Personal/social behavior	Active appreciation

Super Star Runner (Standard 1)

Equipment Needs
Balls or other
throwing objects

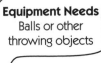

Appropriate for Grades 3-5

- Divide the students into pairs. Each pair gets one throwing object.

- One partner is the thrower. The other partner is the Super Star Runner.

- Both students stand on the starting line. The Super Star Runner runs out to a predetermined line.

- The thrower throws the object to the Super Star Runner to catch. After catching the object, the Super Star Runner runs it back to the thrower. The Super Star Runner then runs back to the line.

- They continue this for about one minute and then trade roles.

- This time they use a different throwing object.

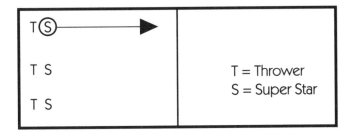

T = Thrower
S = Super Star

GRR-reat Ideas
The below adaptations address the additional standards indicated in the shaded boxes.

Standard 2: Have the pairs discuss the types of throws that would help the Super Star Runner become more successful.

Standard 3: Having the students use a variety of throwing objects helps them gain confidence in throwing and catching. This may also encourage them to play throwing and/or catching games at recess or after school.

Standard 1	Standard 2	Standard 3	Standard 4	Standard 5	Standard 6
Skills and patterns	Learning concepts	Active participation	Physical fitness	Personal/social behavior	Active appreciation

Equipment Needs
Balls, small cones

King Cone (Standard 1)

Appropriate for Grades 3-5

- Divide the students into groups of three. Each group gets one ball and a cone.

- One student in each group guards the cone.

- The other two students pass the ball back and forth to each other and try to hit the cone.

- Switch roles after a set time.

- *Note:* There are a variety of ways to play this game. For example, the game may use 1 guard/3 passers; 2 guards/2 passers; or 2 guards/3 passers. Change the number of players based on the skill and age level of the group. In addition, this game may be played with passes similar to the ones used in basketball or soccer.

GRR-reat Ideas
The below adaptations address the additional standards indicated in the shaded boxes.

Standard 3: Encourage the students to play this activity at recess and add rules to the game.

Standard 1	Standard 2	Standard 3	Standard 4	Standard 5	Standard 6
Skills and patterns	Learning concepts	Active participation	Physical fitness	Personal/social behavior	Active appreciation

Pass Around (Standard 1)

Equipment Needs
Throwing objects

Appropriate for Grades 3-5

- Scatter a variety of objects throughout the gym.

- Have each student find a partner.

- On a signal, each pair tries to successfully pass as many objects as possible during a two-minute period. Each pair must pass an object five times before they can move on to the next one.

- If an object is dropped, the pair leaves it and moves on to another object.

- Repeat this activity to see if the pairs can beat their first scores.

- *Options*:

    o Younger students can work individually on their tossing and catching.

    o Increase the challenge for the older students by adding more passes or increasing the throwing distance.

GRR-reat Ideas
The below adaptations address the additional standards indicated in the shaded boxes.

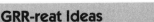

Standard 2: At the completion of the activity, have the partners discuss the basic concepts of throwing and catching (i.e., eyes on the ball; receive into the body; catch using the hands, not the body).

Standard 1	Standard 2	Standard 3	Standard 4	Standard 5	Standard 6
Skills and patterns	Learning concepts	Active participation	Physical fitness	Personal/social behavior	Active appreciation

Equipment Needs
Bouncing balls,
tennis balls

Pro Player (Standard 1)

Appropriate for Grades 3-5

- Divide the students into pairs. Have each pair find a spot in front of a clear wall space.

- Have the pairs practice various ways of catching or fielding a ball off the wall for a predetermined time period. Some ideas are below:

    o One partner throws grounders to the other partner.

    o One partner throws bouncing grounders to the other partner.

    o One partner throws a bouncing grounder and then his or her partner throws a grounder back.

    o Both partners try to catch each other's thrown ball.

    o Partners throw a smaller object (e.g., tennis ball) to catch.

GRR-reat Ideas
The below adaptations address the additional standards indicated in the shaded boxes.

Standard 2: Partners can quiz each other on the proper hand position for catching or fielding a ball below the waist and above the waist.

Standard 1	Standard 2	Standard 3	Standard 4	Standard 5	Standard 6
Skills and patterns	Learning concepts	Active participation	Physical fitness	Personal/social behavior	Active appreciation

Chicken Coop (Standard 1)

Equipment Needs
Spot markers, large basket or bucket, stuffed animals or beanbags

Appropriate for Grades 3-5

- Divide the students into pairs. Give each pair a stuffed animal (or beanbag).

- Place numerous spot markers throughout the gym. Place a large basket or bucket in the middle of the gym.

- The pairs begin the game at one end of the gym. When the game begins, one of the partners runs to any spot marker and tosses his or her stuffed animal at the basket.

- If the stuffed animal goes into the basket, the student takes the spot marker on which he or she is standing, retrieves the stuffed animal, and returns to his or her partner. If he or she misses, the student leaves the spot marker, retrieves the stuffed animal, and returns to his or her partner. The other partner then tries to throw the stuffed animal from any spot marker he or she wishes.

- The game continues until all of the spot markers have been collected.

GRR-reat Ideas
The below adaptations address the additional standards indicated in the shaded boxes.

Standard 2: After playing the game once, allow the students to discuss what would make them more successful. Topics for this discussion may include using a bigger stuffed animal, throwing from the closer spots first, or not throwing when there is someone between them and the basket.

Standard 1	Standard 2	Standard 3	Standard 4	Standard 5	Standard 6
Skills and patterns	Learning concepts	Active participation	Physical fitness	Personal/social behavior	Active appreciation

Equipment Needs
Throwing objects

World Record Catching (Standard 1)

Appropriate for Grades 3-5

- Have each student find a partner.

- Inform the students that they are going to try to set the world record for throwing and catching, and it is very important to make throws that their partners can catch.

- Have the students use a specific throw to toss the ball back and forth for one minute. Tell them to count the number of successful catches.

- Add up the total number of successful catches for the entire class at the end of one minute.

- Repeat the activity to see wether or not the class can beat their record.

GRR-reat Ideas
The below adaptations address the additional standards indicated in the shaded boxes.

Standard 5: Allow pairs to attempt world records with other types of throws and/or catches. Have another pair observe to authenticate the record.

Standard 1	Standard 2	Standard 3	Standard 4	Standard 5	Standard 6
Skills and patterns	Learning concepts	Active participation	Physical fitness	Personal/social behavior	Active appreciation

All-Star Catches (Standard 1)

Equipment Needs
Balls

Appropriate for Grades 3-5

- Have each student find a partner.

- Pairs perform the following activities together to practice the skill of catching:

  o *Hikes/centers*—one partner hikes/centers the ball to the other partner.

  o *Big bounces*—one partner bounces the ball high and the other partner catches ball.

  o *Wall rebounders*—one partner underhand tosses the ball against the wall and the other partner catches the ball after one bounce.

  o *Line drives*—one partner throws the ball against the wall and the other partner catches the ball without a bounce.

  o *Spikes*—one partner throws the ball at the wall and the other partner catches it.

  o *Home runs*—one partner tosses the ball into the air, and the other partner catches it.

  o *Clappers*—one partner tosses the ball into the air and the other partner claps three times before catching it.

GRR-reat Ideas
The below adaptations address the additional standards indicated in the shaded boxes.

Standard 5: Have each student provide positive comments on his or her partner's performance. Offer some ideas for comments, such as "Good job keeping your eye on the ball" or "Way to go on remembering to put your pinkies together when you caught that low ball."

Standard 1	Standard 2	Standard 3	Standard 4	Standard 5	Standard 6
Skills and patterns	Learning concepts	Active participation	Physical fitness	Personal/social behavior	Active appreciation

Equipment Needs
Bouncing balls, CD player, "Wipe Out" on CD

Wipe Out (Standard 1)

Appropriate for Grades 3-5

- Each student gets a ball that bounces.

- When "Wipe Out," by the Beach Boys, begins, the students dribble their balls anywhere in the activity area.

- During the song's drum solo, the students work on various ball-handling activities (e.g., around the waist, figure-eight, toss and catch behind the back).

- Once the drum solo is over, the students start dribbling again. Challenge the students to dribble using their right hands, their left hands, and then alternating hands.

- When the drum solo starts again, the students return to the various ball-handling activities.

GRR-reat Ideas
The below adaptations address the additional standards indicated in the shaded boxes.

Standard 3: Encourage the students to teach or show their ball-handling skills to their siblings, friends, and/or parents.

Standard 1	Standard 2	Standard 3	Standard 4	Standard 5	Standard 6
Skills and patterns	Learning concepts	Active participation	Physical fitness	Personal/social behavior	Active appreciation

Chick Flicks (Standard 1)

Equipment Needs
Rubber chickens, hoops

Appropriate for Grades 3-5

- Divide the class into teams of three. Each team needs several rubber chickens.

- One student on each team is the thrower. The other two students are catchers.

- The two catchers must remain attached at all times and are not allowed to catch the chicken with their hands. To be attached, the catchers may hold hands, stand back-to-back, or grasp forearms. Allow the students some creativity in finding the best ways to stay connected and still catch the chicken.

- The thrower underhand tosses the chicken toward the two catchers.

- Once the catchers have caught the chicken, they must work together to cross the gym to drop the chicken in the chicken coop (hoop).

- Upon completion, the catchers leave the chicken in the hoop and run back to the starting line to try to catch another chicken.

- Play for two minutes and then switch throwers.

- The catchers stand on the starting line at one end of the gym, while the chicken coop (hoop) is placed at the other end of the gym. The thrower stands about halfway between the catchers and the coop (see illustration below).

XX	T	O	
XX	T	O	T = throwers
XX	T	O	X = catchers
			O = hoops

GRR-reat Ideas
The below adaptations address the additional standards indicated in the shaded boxes.

Standard 2: Have the students discuss different strategies that might make them more successful at catching the chicken.

Standard 6: Have the groups create their most creative throw, catch, and carry pattern. Allow half of the groups to demonstrate their patterns, while the other half watches. Repeat so that the groups that were watching now have the chance to demonstrate their patterns.

Standard 1	Standard 2	Standard 3	Standard 4	Standard 5	Standard 6
Skills and patterns	Learning concepts	Active participation	Physical fitness	Personal/social behavior	Active appreciation

Dribbling Antics (Standard 1)

Appropriate for Grades 3-5

- Divide the students into pairs. Give each student a ball and a scarf.

- Below are some skill development ideas:

    o Individually dribble the ball with one hand while tossing the scarf with the other hand.

    o Same as above, but dribble with the nondominant hand.

    o Start dribbling and toss the scarf in the air. Switch dribbling hands before catching the scarf.

    o Dribble with one hand and toss the scarf under a leg. Catch the scarf without stopping the dribble.

    o Place the scarf on top of the ball and underhand toss the ball in the air. Begin to dribble the ball when it returns to the ground and catch the scarf.

    o Dribble through the activity area while tossing and catching the scarf. Each student faces his or her partner and dribbles and self-tosses the scarf.

    o Each student faces his or her partner and dribbles and self-tosses the scarf. Each student slaps his or her thigh before catching the scarf.

GRR-reat Ideas
The below adaptations address the additional standards indicated in the shaded boxes.

Standard 6: Have the pairs create their own patterns of dribbling, tossing, and catching using balls and scarves.

Standard 1	Standard 2	Standard 3	Standard 4	Standard 5	Standard 6
Skills and patterns	Learning concepts	Active participation	Physical fitness	Personal/social behavior	Active appreciation

All-American (Standard 1)

Equipment Needs
Tennis balls,
spot markers

Appropriate for Grades 3-5

- Divide students into pairs. Each pair gets a tennis ball.

- Create a court similar to the one in the picture below by using either the lines on the floor or spot markers.

- The partners should alternate being the batter and the fielder.

- The batter stands in the batter's box and throws the ball against the wall. The ball must bounce once into the batter's box when it comes off the wall.

- The fielder tries to catch the ball.

- If the fielder stops it before the second bounce, the batter does not get any points.

- If the fielder drops the ball or does not catch it before the second bounce, the batter gets the score from whatever area in which the ball lands on the second bounce.

- If the ball lands outside the boundaries, it is an out.

- Each batter gets five throws per inning.

- They play five innings.

	Batter's Box	1 point	2 points	3 points	Home Run
Wall					

GRR-reat Ideas
The below adaptations address the additional standards indicated in the shaded boxes.

Standard 3: Paint or chalk the courts on the playground and set up an All-American tournament for students to play before or after school or even during recess.

Standard 5: At the end of each round, have the students shake hands with their opponents and find new partners to challenge.

Standard 1	Standard 2	Standard 3	Standard 4	Standard 5	Standard 6
Skills and patterns	Learning concepts	Active participation	Physical fitness	Personal/social behavior	Active appreciation

Equipment Needs
Throwing, catching, and kicking objects

Team Create-A-Game (Standard 1)

Appropriate for Grades 3-5

- Create groups of three to four students.

- Provide the groups with specific criteria for creating their own game using designated throwing, catching, and/or kicking skills. The game can focus on just catching, throwing, or kicking or a combination of the skills. Below are sample criteria:

  o The game should demonstrate the ability to throw at a moving target and catch on the move.

  o The game should demonstrate the ability to catch and throw with accuracy and at different speeds.

  o The game should include throwing and catching two different-sized objects.

  o The game should have a beginning and an end.

  o The game should have at least three rules.

- Have each group explain their game to the teacher.

- Allow the students to play their games.

GRR-reat Ideas
The below adaptations address the additional standards indicated in the shaded boxes.

Standard 2: Ask the students to tell what part of their games match a certain stated criteria.

Standard 3: Encourage the students to take their games home and try them with their family members and/or friends.

Standard 6: Allow the students to teach another group about their game creation.

Standard 1	Standard 2	Standard 3	Standard 4	Standard 5	Standard 6
Skills and patterns	Learning concepts	Active participation	Physical fitness	Personal/social behavior	Active appreciation

High-Five Ball (Standard 1)

Equipment Needs
Bouncing balls, clothespins

Appropriate for Grades 3-5

- Divide the students into teams of three. Teams will challenge other teams to a game of High-Five Ball.

- The team with the ball tries to make five successful passes between teammates without having the other team steal the ball.

- If the defenders steal the ball before the offense can get five passes, the defenders begin their quest to get five passes.

- When a team successfully gets five passes, a team member goes to the teacher to get a high-five and a clothespin. That player should clip the clothespin on his or her shirt.

- Teams try to collegt as many clothespins as possible in the allotted time.

- After a certain amount of time, have the teams change opponents.

- If different-colored clothespins are used, math could be integrated into the activity. After the allotted time, have the students count their clothespins. Assign different colors different point values (e.g., a blue pin could be worth 10 points, a red one worth 20 points). Have the students add up their points at the end of the day.

GRR-reat Ideas
The below adaptations address the additional standards indicated in the shaded boxes.

Standard 5: At the end of each round, have the teams change opponents. Before the teams change, have them shake hands with the team they just played. Before starting the new game, have the students shake hands with the team they are about to play and wish them good luck.

Standard 1	Standard 2	Standard 3	Standard 4	Standard 5	Standard 6
Skills and patterns	Learning concepts	Active participation	Physical fitness	Personal/social behavior	Active appreciation

Equipment Needs
Bouncing balls, cones

Dribble Mania (Standard 1)

Appropriate for Grades 3-5

- Have each student find a partner and stand back-to-back with him or her on the center line of the gym.

- Each student places a cone about 10 to 15 yards in front of him or her.

- The pair returns to their starting position, back-to-back, and facing their cones (see diagram below).

- The teacher calls out a task for all of the pairs to complete. After completing the task, each student returns to his or her starting position and holds the balls above his or her head to indicate completion. Each student challenges only his or her partner to complete the directed tasks. If so desired, the partners can keep score of how many points they earn for completing the tasks the quickest.

- Below are some examples of tasks:

  o Dribble to the cone, do 10 jumping jacks, and dribble back.

  o Dribble to the cone, bounce the ball off the wall 5 times, and dribble back.

  o Heel-to-toe walk while dribbling to the cone and back.

  o Roll the ball toward the cone, run to retrieve the ball, touch the cone, and dribble back.

  o Dribble to the cone, move the ball around the waist 10 times, and dribble back.

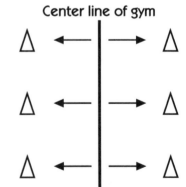

Center line of gym

GRR-reat Ideas
The below adaptations address the additional standards indicated in the shaded boxes.

Standard 6: Have pairs create a task series and then challenge another pair.

Standard 1	Standard 2	Standard 3	Standard 4	Standard 5	Standard 6
Skills and patterns	Learning concepts	Active participation	Physical fitness	Personal/social behavior	Active appreciation

Hoopsters (Standard 1)

Equipment Needs
Hoops, beanbags or yarn balls

Appropriate for Grades 3-5

- Divide the students into pairs. Each pair gets one hoop and two to three beanbags or yarn balls.

- Have the pairs try the following activities. These activities work best if they are performed close to a wall:

  o One partner holds the hoop high and away from his or her body, while the other partner tries to throw a beanbag through it.

  o One partner rolls the hoop along the floor, while the other partner tries to throw a beanbag through it as it rolls.

  o One partner tosses the hoop in the air, while the other partner tries to throw a beanbag through it while it is in the air.

GRR-reat Ideas
The below adaptations address the additional standards indicated in the shaded boxes.

Standard 2: Ask the students about throwing the beanbags through the hoop that is thrown into the air. Is it easier to throw the beanbag through when the hoop is on the way up or on the way down?

Standard 1	Standard 2	Standard 3	Standard 4	Standard 5	Standard 6
Skills and patterns	Learning concepts	Active participation	Physical fitness	Personal/social behavior	Active appreciation

Equipment Needs
Bouncing balls

Big Dog (Standard 1)

Appropriate for Grades 3-5

- Divide the students into groups of three.
- Two of the group members get a ball that bounces.
- The third group member is the leader. The leader's job is to move around the activity area in different pathways, directions, levels, and speeds.
- The other two team members dribble the ball while attempting to follow the leader.
- Let each team member be the leader for a short period of time.

GRR-reat Ideas
The below adaptations address the additional standards indicated in the shaded boxes.

Standard 2: Give a certain parameter to the leaders and ask them to try to get their group members to complete the task. Some examples are 1) Can the leader move in a certain way that makes the group members look like they are doing a lay-up? 2) Can the leader get his or her group members to do a jumping pattern?

Standard 5: Have the two group members thank their leader after each round.

Standard 1	Standard 2	Standard 3	Standard 4	Standard 5	Standard 6
Skills and patterns	Learning concepts	Active participation	Physical fitness	Personal/social behavior	Active appreciation

Four-on-Four Baseball (Standard 1)

Equipment Needs
Spot markers, balls or beanbags

Appropriate for Grades 3-5

• Divide the class into teams of four. Have two teams challenge each other.

• One team is the runners, while the other team is the fielders.

• Set up two very small baseball diamonds using the spot markers as bases. Place each base about 10 feet apart (see diagram below).

• One runner stands at home plate with a ball or beanbag in his or her hand. A large ball that does not go too far when thrown works well. The runner throws the ball into the field.

• A fielder catches or fields the ball and throws or runs it to first base. The ball is then thrown to second, then to third, and finally to home. Whenever the ball passes the runner, the runner must stop.

• At that point, the runner stops on whichever base he or she is closest to and waits for the next runner to throw the ball. One point is scored for every runner that crosses home plate.

• There are no outs. There is no throwing the ball at a runner. The inning is over when all four runners have thrown twice. The fielders and the runners then trade positions.

```
F O          F O              F = fielder
                              X = runner
                    F
   F O      XXXX O            O = base
```

GRR-reat Ideas
The below adaptations address the additional standards indicated in the shaded boxes.

Standard 2: After the first inning, give the teams 30 seconds to strategize about how to better cover the field, make throws, or run the bases.

Standard 1	Standard 2	Standard 3	Standard 4	Standard 5	Standard 6
Skills and patterns	Learning concepts	Active participation	Physical fitness	Personal/social behavior	Active appreciation

CHAPTER 6

A Bird Does Not Sing Because It Has an answer; It Sings Because It Has a Song

Rhythms

All of the activities in this chapter meet Standard One (skills and patterns).
Use the "Tweet Beats" to meet other standards.

Helpful Hints

Rhythms

- Early in the Rhythms unit of a physical education class, introduce some dances in which the students will feel comfortable and gain a level of success.

- Many students will feel somewhat awkward and hesitant about performing rhythmic activities. However, exposing students to a variety of rhythmic activities allows them to become more confident in their rhythmic skills.

- As students become more successful, provide them with a range of physical challenges. Allow them time to create patterns and to demonstrate their new abilities.

- Use the team approach that is used in other physical activities when classes are learning and practicing dances that require small groups. Allow each group to quickly choose a captain for the group. Have the captain review steps or lead the creation process.

- Rhythmic activities and dances are excellent ways to focus on Standards 5 and 6.

Old Macdonald Dance (Standard 1)

Equipment Needs
None

Appropriate for Grades K-2

- Have each student find their own personal space.

- Use the traditional "Old MacDonald Had a Farm" tune, but with some altered words. In the "E-I-E-I-O" part of the song, have the students perform the following motions:
  - o E = Right hand salutes above right eye.
  - o I = Left hand salutes above left eye.
  - o E = Right hand to the stomach.
  - o I = Left hand to the stomach.
  - o O = Cup hands at mouth to make an "O" shape.

- For the song's verse, change the words to the following:
  - o Old MacDonald loved to dance, E-I-E-I-O
  - o And Old MacDonald had some shoulders, E-I-E-I-O
  - o With a shrug, shrug here, and a shrug, shrug there
  - o Here a shrug, there a shrug, everywhere a shrug, shrug
  - o Old MacDonald loved to dance, E-I-E-I-O

- When the students say "shrug," have them shrug their shoulders.

- Below are body parts and motions for other verses:
  - o Hips – boom, boom (i.e., shake the hips)
  - o Knees – knock, knock (i.e., tap the knees together)
  - o Feet – stomp, stomp (i.e., stomp the feet)
  - o Waist – bend, bend (i.e., bend side to side)
  - o Hands – clap, clap (i.e., clap the hands)
  - o Body – wiggle, wiggle (i.e., wiggle the whole body)

Tweet Beat

The below adaptations address the additional standards indicated in the shaded boxes.

Standard 5: Have the students perform some of the movements with a partner. Bending the waist and clapping work the best. Remind the students to thank their partners.

Standard 1	Standard 2	Standard 3	Standard 4	Standard 5	Standard 6
Skills and patterns	Learning concepts	Active participation	Physical fitness	Personal/social behavior	Active appreciation

Equipment Needs
None

Mother Goose Motions (Standard 1)

Appropriate for Grades K-2

Peas Porridge Hot

Peas porridge hot,
Peas porridge cold,
Peas porridge in the pot
Nine days old.

Some like it hot,
Some like it cold,
Some like it in the pot
Nine days old.

Physical Challenges

Perform eight side straddle jumps.

Perform eight forward straddle jumps.

Jack and Jill

Jack and Jill went up the hill
To fetch a pail of water.
Jack fell down and broke his crown
And Jill came tumbling after.

Up Jack got and home did trot
As fast as he could caper
Went to bed and plastered his head
With vinegar and brown paper.

Physical Challenges

Perform eight forward straddle jumps.

Perform eight side straddle jumps.

Perform eight forward straddle jumps.

Perform eight side straddle jumps.

Humpty Dumpty

Humpty Dumpty sat on a wall.
Humpty Dumpty had a great fall.
All the king's horses and all the king's men
Couldn't put Humpty together again!

Physical Challenges

Hop right four times
Hop left four times
Hop right two times, hop left two times
Hop right two times, hop left two times

Tweet Beat
The below adaptations address the additional standards indicated in the shaded boxes.

Standard 5: After the students are able to perform "Peas Porridge Hot," have them find partners. Have them face each other, hold hands, and do the dance.

Standard 1	Standard 2	Standard 3	Standard 4	Standard 5	Standard 6
Skills and patterns	Learning concepts	Active participation	Physical fitness	Personal/social behavior	Active appreciation

Trashin' (Standard 1)

Equipment Needs
CD player, music

Appropriate for Grades 3-5

Music: "Trashin' the Camp" from Walt Disney's *Tarzan*

- Have each student find a partner. The partners stand and face each other.

- *First eight counts*—Each student follows these directions: Hit the partner's right palm, hit the back of partner's right hand, hit partner's left palm, hit the back of partner's left hand, hit the back of partner's two hands, grab partner's two crossed hands, bend at the knees, and jump.

- *Second eight counts*—Each student follows these directions: Slap own thighs, point right index finger, point left index finger, cross the arms, and sway the body four times.

Tweet Beat
The below adaptations address the additional standards indicated in the shaded boxes.

Standard 3: Use this dance as an activity at Parent Night. Have the students bring a parent or other adult out on the floor to teach them this dance pattern.

Standard 5: Have the students tell their partner one reason why he or she was a good partner for this activity.

Standard 1	Standard 2	Standard 3	Standard 4	Standard 5	Standard 6
Skills and patterns	Learning concepts	Active participation	Physical fitness	Personal/social behavior	Active appreciation

Equipment Needs
Spot markers,
CD player, music

Dot Nots (Standard 1)

Appropriate for Grades 3-5

Music: "Popcorn" by Crazy Frog from *Crazy Hits*

- Have each student find a partner. Have each pair get four spot markers.

- Place the spot markers on the floor. Explain the order of the spot markers to the students (see the diagram below).

- Give the students a sequence to practice. A sample sequence might be jumping 1, 2, 3, 4. Have them repeat this sequence several times.

- When the students are successful with the first pattern give them another pattern such as jumping 3, 1, 3, 1, 2, 4, 2, 4.

- When the students know the two patterns, have them put them together to create a longer series. Turn the music on and watch the students dance.

Tweet Beat
The below adaptations address the additional standards indicated in the shaded boxes.

Standard 6: Have the students add different elements, such as various hops, direction changes, and timing changes. Allow each student to create a pattern for his or her partner to attempt.

Standard 1	Standard 2	Standard 3	Standard 4	Standard 5	Standard 6
Skills and patterns	Learning concepts	Active participation	Physical fitness	Personal/social behavior	Active appreciation

Song of the Earth (Standard 1)

Equipment Needs
CD player, short ropes, music

Appropriate for Grades 3-5

Music: "Song of the Earth" by Tom Chapin from *This Pretty Planet*
Formation: Partners facing

- Have each student find a partner and face his or her partner. Give each student two short ropes (8 to 10 inches long). Each student holds a rope in each hand.

- Make a figure-eight to the right of the body with the rope in the right hand (8 counts).

- Make a figure-eight to the left of the body with the rope in the left hand (8 counts).

- Make two figure-eights to the sides of the body with both ropes (8 counts).

- Make two figure-eights in front of the body with both ropes (8 counts).

- Circle the rope in the right hand above the head (8 counts).

- Circle the rope in the left hand above the head (8 counts).

- Circle both ropes above the head (8 counts).

- Circle both ropes in a wheel (i.e., large circles to the sides of the body) (8 counts).

- Have each student dance with his or her partner, point the rope in the right hand toward his or her partner, and do four balances (e.g., step up right, touch left, step back left, touch right) (16 counts).

- Have each student dance with his or her partner, do a right-hand star (i.e., put their right hands together and walk forward in a small circle) and spin the rope in his or her left hand at a low level while walking in the star (16 counts).

- Start the whole dance again.

Tweet Beat
The below adaptations address the additional standards indicated in the shaded boxes.

Standard 6: Take one of the dance actions (e.g., the right-hand star) and change it to a different motion.

Standard 1	Standard 2	Standard 3	Standard 4	Standard 5	Standard 6
Skills and patterns	Learning concepts	Active participation	Physical fitness	Personal/social behavior	Active appreciation

Hawaiian Roller Coaster (Standard 1)

Appropriate for Grades 3-5

Music: "Hawaiian Roller Coaster Ride" from Disney's *Lilo and Stitch*

- Have each student find a partner. Partners face each other.

- At the beginning of the song, there is chanting. Have the students sway until the chanting ends.

- *Part A*: Brush both hands to the side of the body (1 count) and then hit the partner's fists once (i.e., knuckles toward the partner) (1 count). Do this pattern eight times (16 counts).

- *Part B*: Slap the partner's hands twice, hit the partner's fists twice (i.e., knuckles toward the partner), brush the hands across own thighs twice, and hit own fists twice. Part B takes eight counts to perform. Do Part B six times.

- Repeat Part A 16 times (32 counts).

- Repeat Part A and Part B until the music ends.

Tweet Beat
The below adaptations address the additional standards indicated in the shaded boxes.

Standard 5: After the students learn the above pattern, have them perform the dance in groups of four. Partners face one another. One pair begins Part B at the step where they brush their hands across the thighs. The other pair begins the dance at the step where they slap each other's hands. The motions are timed so that the two different motions do not collide.

Standard 1	Standard 2	Standard 3	Standard 4	Standard 5	Standard 6
Skills and patterns	Learning concepts	Active participation	Physical fitness	Personal/social behavior	Active appreciation

Whistle Conga (Standard 1)

Equipment Needs
CD player, music, whistle

Appropriate for Grades 3-5

Music: "Conga" from *20 Jukebox Party Dance Favorites*
or any other conga song

- Have the students practice the conga step pattern individually. The pattern is step right, step left, step right, and then touch the floor on the left side of the body with the left foot. Repeat the activity, but this time begin with the left foot.

- Once the students are able to perform the above pattern, the teacher blows a whistle. The number of times the whistle is blown equals the number of students who should be in each group performing the conga pattern. Each group dances in a line with students placing their hands on the shoulders of the person in front of them.

- One whistle blow indicates that the students should start dancing solo again.

Tweet Beat
The below adaptations address the additional standards indicated in the shaded boxes.

Standard 3: Host a family dance night where the students teach their parents this dance.

Standard 5: Near the end of the dance, try to get all of the students in one conga line.

Standard 1	Standard 2	Standard 3	Standard 4	Standard 5	Standard 6
Skills and patterns	Learning concepts	Active participation	Physical fitness	Personal/social behavior	Active appreciation

Equipment Needs
CD player, music

Cowboy Slap Dance (Standard 1)

Appropriate for Grades 3-5

Music: "We Are Family" by Sister Sledge
on *Radio Disney Jams Volume 2*
Formation: Double circle with partners facing

- *Part A*: Slap partner's palms twice and slap own thighs twice. Repeat this pattern three more times (16 counts).

- *Part B*: Slide clockwise three times and slap partner's right hand (4 counts). Slide counterclockwise three times and slap partner's left hand (4 counts). Repeat Part B.

- *Part C*: Do-si-do partner for six counts and clap own hands twice (counts 7, 8). Repeat Part C three more times.

Tweet Beat
The below adaptations address the additional standards indicated in the shaded boxes.

Standard 5: At the conclusion of the dance, remind the students to thank their partner for the dance. In addition, have each pair find another pair. Students introduce their partner to the other pair and exchange partners.

Standard 1	Standard 2	Standard 3	Standard 4	Standard 5	Standard 6
Skills and patterns	Learning concepts	Active participation	Physical fitness	Personal/social behavior	Active appreciation

One-Step Mixer (Standard 1)

Equipment Needs
CD player, music

Appropriate for Grades 3-5

Music: "Disney Mambo No. 5" by Lou Bega
from *Radio Disney Jams Volume 2*
Formation: Double circle with partners facing counterclockwise

- The students take eight steps forward moving counterclockwise around the circle (8 counts).

- The students take two side steps away from the center of the circle (i.e., step right, close left, step right, close left) (4 counts) and then take two side steps toward the center of the circle (i.e., step left, close right, step left, close right) (4 counts).

- Facing each other, the partners take four steps away from each other (4 counts). The partners then take four steps toward each other and high-five on the fourth step (4 counts).

- Facing each other, the partners take four steps away from each other (4 counts). The student on the inner circle then takes four steps toward the partner, while the partner on the outer circle moves forward four steps to the next student (4 counts).

- Everyone begins the dance again with a new partner.

Tweet Beat
The below adaptations address the additional standards indicated in the shaded boxes.

Standard 3: Have the fifth graders teach this dance to the third graders and act as the third graders' partners.

Standard 5: The students on the inner circle welcome their new partner by saying "hello," when the students from the outer circle move forward.

Standard 1	Standard 2	Standard 3	Standard 4	Standard 5	Standard 6
Skills and patterns	Learning concepts	Active participation	Physical fitness	Personal/social behavior	Active appreciation

Yellow Rose of Texas (Standard 1)

Appropriate for Grades 3-5

Music: "Yellow Rose of Texas"

- Have each student find a partner.

- Have each student promenade with his or her partner anywhere in the activity area (16 counts). During the last few counts of these 16 counts, each pair finds another pair to form a group of four.

- Each group of four circles to their left (8 counts), walks into the center of their small circle (4 counts), and then back out (4 counts). Each group now circles to their right (8 counts), walks into the center of their small circle (4 counts), and then back out (4 counts).

- The group performs a right-hand star (8 counts) and then a left-hand star (8 counts).

- The pairs do-si-do their partners and then their corners.

- Each student takes the corner person as his or her new partner and starts the dance over.

Tweet Beat
The below adaptations address the additional standards indicated in the shaded boxes.

Standard 2: Before starting the dance, have the partners review various dance motions (e.g., promenade, do-si-do, swing, right-hand star).

Standard 1	Standard 2	Standard 3	Standard 4	Standard 5	Standard 6
Skills and patterns	Learning concepts	Active participation	Physical fitness	Personal/social behavior	Active appreciation

Octopus Dance (Standard 1)

Equipment Needs
Exercise tubing,
CD player, music

Appropriate for Grades 3-5

Music: "Octopus' Garden" from *Finding Nemo Ocean Favorites*

- Have each student find a partner and have them face each other. Each student gets an exercise tube and stands on his or her own tubing, holding the ends of his or her partner's tubing.

- *Part A:* Pull both ends of the tubing forward and backward (16 counts).

- *Part B:* Move the tubing in a motion similar to cross country skiing (16 counts).

- *Part C:* Push both ends of the tubing out and in (16 counts).

- *Part D:* Stretch the tubing while lifting one leg and then the other leg (16 counts).

- Repeat all four parts again.

- Each pair side steps (i.e., step left, close right) in a circle, while doing biceps curls (32 counts).

- Begin the entire dance again.

Tweet Beat
The below adaptations address the additional standards indicated in the shaded boxes.

Standard 2: Have the students figure out the best way to move without letting the tubing slip out from underneath their feet.

Standard 1	Standard 2	Standard 3	Standard 4	Standard 5	Standard 6
Skills and patterns	Learning concepts	Active participation	Physical fitness	Personal/social behavior	Active appreciation

Equipment Needs
CD player, music

Teamwork Dance (Standard 1)

Appropriate for Grades 4-6

Music: "Shake Your Groove Thing" by Peaches and Herb
Formation: Group of three facing another group of three

- The trios take three steps forward and give a highten to the groups in front of them (4 counts). The trios take three steps backward and clap (4 counts). Repeat the forward and backward movement again.

- The center student in each trio performs a right elbow swing with the partner on his or her left (8 counts).

- The center student in each trio performs a left elbow swing with the partner on the right (8 counts).

- The two groups of three join hands and circle to their left for 16 counts.

- The group of six drops their hands and splits back into two trios again. Each trio parades (i.e., turn to the left to form a line of three and follow the leader) around the activity area for eight counts.

- Each trio now parades in the opposite direction (8 counts).

- The dance starts over.

Tweet Beat
The below adaptations address the additional standards indicated in the shaded boxes.

Standard 5: At the end of the dance, have the center student compliment the other two dancers in his or her group.

Standard 1	Standard 2	Standard 3	Standard 4	Standard 5	Standard 6
Skills and patterns	Learning concepts	Active participation	Physical fitness	Personal/social behavior	Active appreciation

CHAPTER 7

It Is Impossible to Keep a Straight Face in the Presence of One or More Kittens

Fitness

All of the activities in this chapter meet Standard One (skills and patterns) and Standard Four (physical fitness). Use the "Cat Nips" to meet other standards.

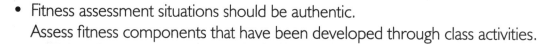

Helpful Hints

Fitness

- Work on health-related fitness parameters as much as possible. If the primary activity of the lesson focuses on cardiovascular fitness, use the warm-up and cool-down times to work other health-related fitness parameters (e.g., muscular strength, muscular endurance, flexibility, body composition).

- When working on fitness components, if possible, try to use game-like activities. Given the choice, students usually prefer games rather than drills, warm-ups, or assessment.

- Fitness assessment situations should be authentic. Assess fitness components that have been developed through class activities.

- Expose students to as many activities as possible related to fitness components. In this way, the students can find activities that they enjoy and can do outside of school and later in life.

- Find a simple way to assess the exertion levels of the students. One way is the "Zoom Zone" format. Place posters of each of the "Zoom Zone" exertion levels on the wall. Be sure to space each of these far enough away from the other two so that all of the students have room to stand by one of the posters. After an activity, have each student stand by the poster that best represents his or her level of exertion. By doing this, the teacher can easily assess the students' levels of perceived exertion. A chart of these levels follows below and is also illustrated on the next page.

  1. Slimed (very low level of perceived exertion)

  2. Zoom Zone (good level of perceived exertion)

  3. Red Alert (very high level of perceived exertion)

SLIMED

(low level of perceived exertion)

ZOOM ZONE

(good level of perceived exertion)

RED ALERT

(very high level of perceived exertion)

Equipment Needs
Cones, animal pictures

Animal Fitness Trail (Standards 1 & 4)

Appropriate for Grades K-2

- Place cones around the gym and attach pictures of animals to each cone.

- Students move from cone to cone by way of animal movements. For example, if the first cone has a picture of a bear, the student moves to the next cone using a bear crawl. If the next cone has a picture of a crab, the student changes his or her movement to a crab walk and moves on to the next cone.

- Other possible movements could include actions such as a frog jump, alligator crawl, kangaroo jump, elephant stomp, or gorilla gallop.

Cat Nips
The below adaptations address the additional standards indicated in the shaded boxes.

Standard 5: Reinforce to the students that the goal is not to perform the movements as fast as possible, but instead to perform the motions in the best possible form.

Standard 6: Allow the students to choose their three best animal motions. Have half of the class demonstrate their motions for the other half. Repeat so that the other half of the class has an opportunity to demonstrate their movements. This is a good time to teach about appreciating others' efforts. Applause is one of those ways.

Standard 1	Standard 2	Standard 3	Standard 4	Standard 5	Standard 6
Skills and patterns	Learning concepts	Active participation	Physical fitness	Personal/social behavior	Active appreciation

Shark Attack (Standards 1 & 4)

Equipment Needs
Spot markers,
hoops, dice

Appropriate for Grades K-2

- Make a circle around the gym using spot markers and hoops (see sample diagram below).

- Have each student find a partner and give each pair a die.

- The pairs can start at any spot on the circle. One student from each pair rolls the die, and whatever number appears on the die represents the number of spots they move forward.

- If the pair lands on a spot marker, they do a teacher-stated activity (e.g., 10 swimming arms, 10 hops, 10 front punches, or other appropriate activity).

- If the pair lands in a hoop (i.e., shark's pond), they run one lap around the circle and return to the hoop for their next roll. Remind them to take their die with them when they run.

Cat Nips
The below adaptations address the additional standards indicated in the shaded boxes.

Standard 5: Have the pair determine a fair way to choose who rolls the die.

Standard 1	Standard 2	Standard 3	Standard 4	Standard 5	Standard 6
Skills and patterns	Learning concepts	Active participation	Physical fitness	Personal/social behavior	Active appreciation

Equipment Needs
Scarves

Race Cars (Standards 1 & 4)

Appropriate for Grades K-2

- Have each student find a partner.

- Give two scarves to one of the partners. This student is the walking partner. The walking partner walks clockwise on the inner circle of the "race track."

- The other partner is the race car driver. He or she runs counterclockwise on the outer circle of the track. As the race car driver passes his or her partner each lap, he or she takes one of the scarves from the partner.

- When the race car driver has both scarves, he or she has completed the race and becomes the new walking partner.

- The old walking partner now becomes the new race car driver and he or she begins to run around the race track.

Cat Nips
The below adaptations address the additional standards indicated in the shaded boxes.

Standard 2: After the activity is completed, have the partners discuss the best way to hand off a scarf in order to keep the runner from having to slow down.

Standard 1	Standard 2	Standard 3	Standard 4	Standard 5	Standard 6
Skills and patterns	Learning concepts	Active participation	Physical fitness	Personal/social behavior	Active appreciation

Ghostbusters (Standards 1 & 4)

Equipment Needs
Spot markers, CD player, music

Appropriate for Grades K-2

Music: "Ghostbusters" by Ray Parker, Jr. on *Radio Disney Kid Jams*

- Place spot markers in a circle on the floor. Use only enough spot markers so that about one-third of the class has a spot to stand on.

- The remaining students position themselves around the outside of the circle. These students are the runners.

- Every time the students hear the word "Ghostbusters," the students on the spot markers must leave their spots to become runners. All of the runners must quickly try to find a spot to get on. Only one student is allowed on each spot. These students cannot return to the same spot marker.

- The students who do not find a spot must keep running.

- At any time during the activity, the teacher may call out "Ghostbusters."

Cat Nips
The below adaptations address the additional standards indicated in the shaded boxes.

Standard 5: Often two students will end up on a spot at the same time. Determine before the activity begins whether it is "tall day" or "short day." If it is a tall day, then the taller of the two students gets the spot. If it is short day, then the shorter of the two students gets the spot.

Standard 1	Standard 2	Standard 3	Standard 4	Standard 5	Standard 6
Skills and patterns	Learning concepts	Active participation	Physical fitness	Personal/social behavior	Active appreciation

Equipment Needs
CD player, music, flash cards

Flash Card Fitness (Standards 1 & 4)

Appropriate for Grades 3-5

- Have the students jog around the activity area while the music plays. When the music stops, each student freezes. Read aloud a flash card and have the students perform the stated activity. Below are some sample activities:

    o *Bug body*—lie on the back and shake arms and legs in the air.

    o *Touchdown*—pretend to carry a football and jog in place.

    o *Trojan push-ups*—hold the "up" position of a push-up and alternately touch the shoulders with the opposite hands.

    o *Crab kicks*—assume the crab-walk position and alternately kick legs in the air.

    o *Volleyball block*—jump up and pretend to perform a volleyball block.

    o *Slam dunks*—jump up and pretend to make elaborate basketball dunks.

- Have each student find a partner. One partner positions him or herself somewhere on the lap path. Give each of these students an activity flash card. The other partner is the runner. Have all of the runners start running around the lap path. When time is called, each runner goes to the closest card holder and performs the activity on the card. When the teacher says "change," the runners take the cards and the other students begin to run.

Cat Nips
The below adaptations address the additional standards indicated in the shaded boxes.

Standard 5: Have each student find a partner and have them encourage each other by saying supportive phrases like, "Way to go!" or "Awesome job!"

Standard 1	Standard 2	Standard 3	Standard 4	Standard 5	Standard 6
Skills and patterns	Learning concepts	Active participation	Physical fitness	Personal/social behavior	Active appreciation

Traffic Trainer (Standards 1 & 4)

Equipment Needs
None

Appropriate for Grades 3-5

- Have the students randomly move around the activity area using a specified locomotor skill.

- When the teacher calls "red light," the students freeze and listen to the traffic direction (examples below). The students perform the stated traffic direction.

- After an allotted time, the teacher calls "green light" and a new locomotor skill. The students perform this skill until the teacher calls "red light" again.

- Below are some sample traffic directions:

    o *Park*—sit on the floor with heels touching ground in front of body and stretch.

    o *Flat tire*—hold the "up" position of a push-up.

    o *Brake*—stand with the right heel touching floor in front of body and stretch.

    o *Reverse*—slowly move backward.

    o *Curve*—lean to the right and left while walking in a curved line.

    o *Accelerate*—move feet in place quickly.

    o *Bumpy road*—gallop to the wall and back.

    o *School zone*—walk.

- Once the students know the traffic directions, call out the traffic directions faster and give them a series of directions before calling "green light" again.

Cat Nips
The below adaptations address the additional standards indicated in the shaded boxes.

Standard 3: Provide the students with "traffic tickets" that list all of the traffic directions and instruct them to take them home to demonstrate each of the activities to their families.

Standard 1	Standard 2	Standard 3	Standard 4	Standard 5	Standard 6
Skills and patterns	Learning concepts	Active participation	Physical fitness	Personal/social behavior	Active appreciation

Equipment Needs
Small index cards, cones, CD player, music

Crazy Colors (Standards 1 & 4)

Appropriate for Grades 3-5

- Mark the index cards as specified below:
  - o Six cards marked with the word "Red."
  - o Six cards marked with the word "Green."
  - o Six cards marked with the word "Purple."
  - o Six cards marked with the word "Orange."
  - o Six cards marked with the word "Yellow."
  - o Six cards marked with the word "Blue."

- Place different colored cones in a scattered formation throughout the gymnasium. Spread the cones out as far as possible.

- Under each cone, place one of the index cards. Be sure not to put a color card under a cone of the same color (i.e., a card that reads "Red" should not be placed under a red cone).

- Each student finds a spot in general space.

- When the music begins, the students jog (or any other locomotor skill) to any cone and look under it. They read the card and replace the cone directly over the card and then jog to a cone of the color specified on the card. For example, if the card says "Green," the student jogs to a green cone.

- At the end of a minute, have the students feel for their heart rates and discuss why their hearts are beating faster and why it is healthy to get their hearts to beat faster.

- Repeat the activity several times.

- Another idea for this activity is to have students perform one sit-up at each cone before looking under the cone for the index card.

Cat Nips
The below adaptations address the additional standards indicated in the shaded boxes.

Standard 5: Have each student high-five three different students while moving from cone to cone.

Standard 1	Standard 2	Standard 3	Standard 4	Standard 5	Standard 6
Skills and patterns	Learning concepts	Active participation	Physical fitness	Personal/social behavior	Active appreciation

Veins and Arteries (Standards 1 & 4)

Equipment Needs
None

Appropriate for Grades 3-5

- Tell the students that the gym is their body and that the lines on the gym floor are their veins and arteries.

- Assign several students to be the taggers and tell them that taggers represent risk factors for heart disease. The other students move along the veins and arteries.

- Using a fast walk, all of the students move only along the lines on the gym floor. When a student is tagged by a tagger, he or she becomes a "blockage" in the vein or artery. The blockages must put themselves in an inverted "V" position over a line on the gym floor. The blockages remain in the inverted "V" position for a count of 20 (or other appropriate time limit) and then return to the game.

- If students who are still moving around come to a blockage, they must crawl under the blockage (i.e., the inverted "V") to continue moving.

- Switch taggers after a set time.

Cat Nips
The below adaptations address the additional standards indicated in the shaded boxes.

Standard 2: Discuss the risk factors for heart disease (e.g., obesity, cholesterol, diet high in fat, inactivity, smoking) and how blockages in the veins and arteries can lead to heart attacks.

Standard 1	Standard 2	Standard 3	Standard 4	Standard 5	Standard 6
Skills and patterns	Learning concepts	Active participation	Physical fitness	Personal/social behavior	Active appreciation

Equipment Needs
Bowling pins or tennis ball cans, tennis balls

Bowling For Fitness (Standards 1 & 4)

Appropriate for Grades 3-5

- Give each student a tennis ball and a bowling pin or empty tennis ball can.

- Students try to protect their pin while moving around a small activity area trying to knock down other students' pins.

- Balls should only be rolled.

- Once a student's pin is knocked down, he or she leaves the pin down and moves to the side to perform a fitness task previously specified by the teacher. Examples for fitness tasks might include crunches, push-ups, jumping jacks, and jogging a lap. Select a task appropriate for the age group.

- After completing the fitness task, the student returns his or her pin to the standing position and rejoins the game.

- *Hint*: The teacher should change the fitness task often.

Cat Nips
The below adaptations address the additional standards indicated in the shaded boxes.

Standard 2: Instead of going to an area with posted fitness activities, a student must come to the teacher. The teacher states a health-related fitness component, and the student demonstrates an activity or motion related to the stated component before he or she may return to the game.

Standard 1	Standard 2	Standard 3	Standard 4	Standard 5	Standard 6
Skills and patterns	Learning concepts	Active participation	Physical fitness	Personal/social behavior	Active appreciation

Fit and Go (Standards 1 & 4)

Equipment Needs
Signs, station equipment, CD player, music

Appropriate for Grades 3-5

- Prior to the activity, post circuit station signs around the activity area and place appropriate equipment at each station.

- Have each student find a partner and go to a station.

- When the music begins, the pairs perform the activity posted at the station.

- After a short amount of time (e.g., 45 seconds), stop the music. When the music stops, the pairs run a lap around the activity area. Upon completion of the lap, the pairs move to the next station.

- Repeat until all stations are completed.

- Below are some examples of possible stations:

    o Jump rope
    o Push-ups
    o Box steps
    o Crunches
    o Jumping jacks
    o Crab walk
    o Lunges
    o Slides
    o Bicep curls
    o Jogging in place
    o Dribbling while jogging in place

Cat Nips
The below adaptations address the additional standards indicated in the shaded boxes.

Standard 2: At each station, have a list of the health-related fitness components. Before each pair begins running their lap, have them touch the component associated with the activity they just completed.

Standard 1	Standard 2	Standard 3	Standard 4	Standard 5	Standard 6
Skills and patterns	Learning concepts	Active participation	Physical fitness	Personal/social behavior	Active appreciation

Equipment Needs
None

Face Up, Face Down (Standards 1 & 4)

Appropriate for Grades 3-5

- Have all of the students begin in the crab-walk position. This is "face up." Have the students perform 10 glut slaps (i.e., slap the gluteus maximus with alternating hands).

- Have the students assume the push-up position. This is "face down." Have the students do 10 Trojan push-ups (i.e., alternately touching the right hand to the left shoulder and then the left hand to the right shoulder).

- Each time the students complete a "face up, face down" series, the number of required motions is reduced by two (10, 8, 6, 4, and finally 2).

- This activity may need to be adapted to the students' fitness level. For example, the students may start with four "face up, face downs" instead of 10.

Cat Nips
The below adaptations address the additional standards indicated in the shaded boxes.

Standard 2: Have the students identify the muscles they used during this activity.

Standard 3: Encourage the students to do this activity every night before they go to bed for one week. Ask them about it during class time in order to reinforce the idea.

Standard 1	Standard 2	Standard 3	Standard 4	Standard 5	Standard 6
Skills and patterns	Learning concepts	Active participation	Physical fitness	Personal/social behavior	Active appreciation

Fitness Playbook (Standards 1 & 4)

Equipment Needs
Playbooks, balls, beanbags, balloons

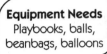

Appropriate for Grades 3-5

- Have the class divide into teams of three to four players.

- Each team chooses a team captain who gets a fitness playbook from the teacher. A sample of a playbook is below..

- The teams perform all of the activities in the playbook (in any order).

- Any team that finishes early should "run the option."

Fitness Playbook

PLAY	INSTRUCTIONS
Kickoff	Each team member leads the team in a stretch.
Run	The team jogs one lap around the gym.
Pass	Team members pass a ball back and forth with each other while sliding up and down the gym floor.
Audible	Shout "I love P.E." 10 times.
Touchdown	In the push-up position, team members pass the ball around in a circle five times.
Extra Point	Team members run a lap and do a touchdown dance at the end of the lap.
Field Goal	In the crab-walk position, each team member dribbles a bean bag with his or her feet to half court and back.
Punt	Each team member punts a balloon seven times.
Option	Each team member runs to touch a wall, returns, and then huddles as a team. Repeat this play, sending team members to a different wall each time.

Cat Nips
The below adaptations address the additional standards indicated in the shaded boxes.

Standard 5: After a team runs the option three times, have the team huddle together to decide which three plays they will try again.

Standard 1	Standard 2	Standard 3	Standard 4	Standard 5	Standard 6
Skills and patterns	Learning concepts	Active participation	Physical fitness	Personal/social behavior	Active appreciation

Equipment Needs
Activity directions,
jump ropes

Pal Patterns (Standards 1 & 4)

Appropriate for Grades 3-5

- Place activity directions at various positions throughout the gym.

- Have each student find a partner and go to an activity direction site.

- Pairs read the activity directions and complete them in order.

- Below are some sample activity directions:

  o Jog a lap going in the opposite direction from partner.
  o Jog a lap together.
  o Do four back-to-back get-ups (i.e., back-to-back with elbows hooked).
  o Jog a lap going in the opposite direction from partner.
  o Do partner wall push-ups (i.e., one partner does a push-up against the wall, while the other partner lightly leans on the performing partner's back to offer resistance). Each partner does five push-ups.
  o Jog an "X" across the gym.
  o Do 10 partner high-five curl-ups (i.e., partners sit facing each other where they both do a curl-up and give each other a high-five).
  o Jog a lap going in the opposite direction from partner.
  o Do 15 face-to-face jump ropes.
  o Do 15 side-by-side jump ropes.
  o Jog a lap going in the opposite direction from partner.

Cat Nips
The below adaptations address the additional standards indicated in the shaded boxes.

Standard 6: After completing all of the activities, have each pair practice a chosen activity from the above list and demonstrate it for another pair.

Standard 1	Standard 2	Standard 3	Standard 4	Standard 5	Standard 6
Skills and patterns	Learning concepts	Active participation	Physical fitness	Personal/social behavior	Active appreciation

Abs and Sets (Standards 1 & 4)

Equipment Needs
Balls

Appropriate for Grades 3-5

- Have each student find a partner.

- One partner lies on his or her back and performs curl-ups.

- The other partner stands by the performing partner's head and holds a ball.

- When the performing partner does a curl-up, the standing partner drops the ball straight down so that the performing partner can catch and toss the ball straight back up to the standing partner.

- Repeat this sequence for 30 to 60 seconds and then have the partners switch positions.

- Continue until each student has done curl-ups three times.

Cat Nips
The below adaptations address the additional standards indicated in the shaded boxes.

Standard 2: Have each pair review the proper technique of a curl-up before beginning the activity.

Standard 1	Standard 2	Standard 3	Standard 4	Standard 5	Standard 6
Skills and patterns	Learning concepts	Active participation	Physical fitness	Personal/social behavior	Active appreciation

Equipment Needs
Dynabands®, beanbags, mats or step benches

Fitness Relay (Standards 1 & 4)

Appropriate for Grades 3-5

- Have the class divide into groups of four.

- Each student in a group begins at a different station. Each group selects a runner who will begin at Station 1, while each of the other group members will start at one of the remaining stations.

- When the runner completes Station 1, he or she advances to Station 2. The student at Station 2 moves to Station 3 and the student at Station 3 moves to Station 4. Finally, the student at Station 4 moves to Station 1 and becomes the new runner.

- Below are some ideas for stations:

   o *Station 1*: Run two laps.

   o *Station 2*: Side-arm pulls with a Dynaband®.

   o *Station 3*: Step-ups (i.e., using an unfolded mat or a step bench, the student steps up and down).

   o *Station 4*: Beanbag curl-ups (i.e., with one beanbag in each hand, the student does a curl-up and puts the beanbags on his or her knees, lies back down, does another curl-up, and retrieves the beanbags).

- Have the groups repeat this relay for a predetermined number of times or for a specific amount of time.

Cat Nips
The below adaptations address the additional standards indicated in the shaded boxes.

Standard 2: After the students have completed the activity, have them review the health-related fitness components while they stretch.

Standard 1	Standard 2	Standard 3	Standard 4	Standard 5	Standard 6
Skills and patterns	Learning concepts	Active participation	Physical fitness	Personal/social behavior	Active appreciation

Jump Rope Pyramid (Standards 1 & 4)

Equipment Needs
CD player, music, jump ropes

Appropriate for Grades 3-5

- When the music begins, the students start to jump rope. When the music stops, have the students stretch using a stretch of their choice.

- Use the following pyramid-like time sequence:

  - Jump rope for 15 seconds
  - Stretch for 15 seconds
  - Jump rope for 30 seconds
  - Stretch for 15 seconds
  - Jump rope for 45 seconds
  - Stretch for 15 seconds
  - Jump rope for 60 seconds
  - Stretch for 15 seconds
  - Jump rope for 45 seconds
  - Stretch for 15 seconds
  - Jump rope for 30 seconds
  - Stretch for 15 seconds
  - Jump rope for 15 seconds
  - Stretch for 15 seconds

- This sequence may be repeated in order to develop endurance.

Cat Nips
The below adaptations address the additional standards indicated in the shaded boxes.

Standard 2: Have the students explain the difference between muscular endurance and cardiovascular endurance.

Standard 1	Standard 2	Standard 3	Standard 4	Standard 5	Standard 6
Skills and patterns	Learning concepts	Active participation	Physical fitness	Personal/social behavior	Active appreciation

Fitness Chase (Standards 1 & 4)

Appropriate for Grades 3-5

- Make activity cards that list various fitness activities. Examples might include 10 jumping jacks, 5 crunches, 5 push-ups, or 10 mountain climbers.

- Select four students to be chasers (or an appropriate amount for the size of the class). The remaining students are runners.

- Give each chaser a fitness activity card.

- When a chaser tags a runner, the chaser gives the activity card to the runner. The runner performs the activity on the card and the two students switch roles so that the tagged runner becomes a chaser and the chaser becomes a runner.

- Students cannot be tagged while performing an activity.

- Have the students check their heart rates before and after the activity and discuss with them the relationship between intensity and heart rate.

Cat Nips
The below adaptations address the additional standards indicated in the shaded boxes.

Standard 2: Write a muscle name on each of the activity cards. When a student is tagged, he or she must perform an activity associated with that muscle.

Standard 1	Standard 2	Standard 3	Standard 4	Standard 5	Standard 6
Skills and patterns	Learning concepts	Active participation	Physical fitness	Personal/social behavior	Active appreciation

Disaster Area (Standards 1 & 4)

Equipment Needs
Jump bands, cones, golf tubes, mats, jump ropes, spot markers

Appropriate for Grades 3-5

- Divide the class into three groups of students. Give each group a color name (e.g., red, blue, and green).

- Set up various stations in a circular fashion around the gym (disaster area). Below are some ideas for the stations:

  o *Snow skiing*—jump over jump bands stretched over cones.

  o *Leaping rivers*—leap over golf tubes held by other students.

  o *Jumping off the mountain*—jump off folded mats.

  o *Snake pit*—jump over jump ropes spun slowly by other students.

  o *Island hopping*—jump on each spot marker.

  o *Hail storm*—catch balls thrown by other students.

  o *Swinging bridge*—jump five times over a rope that two students are swaying back and forth.

- Have two of the groups (e.g., red and blue teams) travel twice through the disaster area before meeting the teacher in the middle of the activity area. The other group of students (e.g., green team) are disaster helpers who help run the disaster area by performing various tasks, such as tossing balls, turning ropes, and holding equipment.

- The blue and green teams switch places so that the red and green teams now travel through the disaster area while the blue team assists.

Cat Nips
The below adaptations address the additional standards indicated in the shaded boxes.

Standard 5: Have the students that are becoming the new disaster helpers help restore the area by retrieving balls and positioning cones, spot markers, and hoops.

Standard 1	Standard 2	Standard 3	Standard 4	Standard 5	Standard 6
Skills and patterns	Learning concepts	Active participation	Physical fitness	Personal/social behavior	Active appreciation

Equipment Needs
Checklists, pencils, jump ropes

Fit Fun (Standards 1 & 4)

Appropriate for Grades 3-5

- Create a Fit Fun Checklist similar to the example below.

- Give each student a checklist and a pencil.

- Students move throughout the activity area performing each of the activities with a different partner. The partner then signs his or her name on the checklist indicating in which activity he or she participated.

- Have each student monitor his or her heart rate and perceived exertion during the activity

FIT FUN CHECKLIST

Exercise	Partner
10 Partner High-Five Push-Ups	
Fast Walk 2 Laps	
20 Curl-Ups	
25 Jumping Jacks	
15 Push-Ups in Crab Walk Position	
25 Line Jumps	
10 Push-Ups	
30 Jump Ropes	
Jog 2 Laps	
Each Partner Leads 3 Stretches	

Cat Nips
The below adaptations address the additional standards indicated in the shaded boxes.

Standard 3: Send a copy of the checklist home with each student. Have the students complete the checklist with a friend, sibling, or other family member. Require parents to sign the checklist before a student can return it.

Standard 5: Have the students give a high-five to their exercise partner before moving on to a new partner.

Standard 1	Standard 2	Standard 3	Standard 4	Standard 5	Standard 6
Skills and patterns	Learning concepts	Active participation	Physical fitness	Personal/social behavior	Active appreciation

King of the Jungle (Standards 1 & 4)

Equipment Needs
Small stuffed animals or beanbags, large stuffed animals

Appropriate for Grades 3-5

- Divide the students into teams of three. Give each team a small stuffed animal (or beanbag).

- Organize the teams in a circle (see diagram below). Place three to four larger stuffed animals at the center of the circle.

- Have each team decide who from their team will be the first, second, and third runners.

- On "Go," the first runner for each team starts running around the circle carrying their small stuffed animal.

- Upon returning to the team's starting point, the first runner hands off the stuffed animal to the next runner, who now runs a lap around the circle and hands off to the third runner.

- When the third runner returns to the team's starting point, he or she hands the stuffed animal to the first runner. The first runner runs to the center of the circle to capture one of the larger stuffed animals.

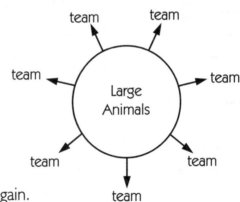

- The first three teams to get a large stuffed animal win a point.

- Have the teams rotate their running orders and play again.

Cat Nips

The below adaptations address the additional standards indicated in the shaded boxes.

Standard 2: Allow the teams 15 to 30 seconds to determine a strategy that is best for handing off the stuffed animal.

Standard 5: Reinforce the importance of runners not running into other runners while handing off. In addition, remind the students that it is not positive social behavior to trip others, steal stuffed animals from others' hands, or shove other students.

Standard 1	Standard 2	Standard 3	Standard 4	Standard 5	Standard 6
Skills and patterns	Learning concepts	Active participation	Physical fitness	Personal/social behavior	Active appreciation

Equipment Needs
Long jump ropes

Queen Bee (Standards 1 & 4)

Appropriate for Grades 3-5

- Divide the students into groups of four.

- Two of the group members are turners. The other two students are jumpers. One is the Queen Bee and the other is the worker bee.

- The Queen Bee jumps in a certain pattern. The teacher may wish to put parameters on the pattern, such as it cannot have more than 10 jumps.

- The worker bee must jump the same pattern as demonstrated by the Queen Bee.

- If the worker bee is able to repeat the Queen Bee's pattern without any misses, the worker bee becomes the new Queen Bee. The old Queen Bee becomes a rope turner and one of the rope turners becomes the new worker bee.

- If the worker bee cannot perform the pattern without any misses, the Queen Bee remains the leader and offers a new pattern.

- *Note:* After three unsuccessful attempts by the worker bee, it may be appropriate to have a mandatory change of the Queen Bee.

Cat Nips
The below adaptations address the additional standards indicated in the shaded boxes.

Standard 5: Have the Queen Bee give the worker bee a high-five if he or she is able to complete the pattern successfully.

Standard 1	Standard 2	Standard 3	Standard 4	Standard 5	Standard 6
Skills and patterns	Learning concepts	Active participation	Physical fitness	Personal/social behavior	Active appreciation

Clock (Standards 1 & 4)

Appropriate for Grades 3-5

- Divide the class into groups of five to six students. Each group gets a long jump rope.

- Two group members turn the rope, while the other members of the group stand in line to jump.

- The object of the activity is to jump all 12 hours (1:00, 2:00, 3:00, etc.) by running into the middle of the turning rope, jumping the correct number of times, and then running out, without missing a jump.

- After jumping the correct number of times, the jumper runs out and goes to the end of the line.

- Players continue increasing the number of jumps, going from 1 to 12 jumps. If a jumper misses a jump, he or she changes places with one of the turners.

- There cannot be any rope turns or hesitations when switching jumpers. The transition from one jumper to the next must be seamless. The jumpers must work together to to get from 1 to 12 without a miss.

Cat Nips
The below adaptations address the additional standards indicated in the shaded boxes.

Standard 5: Remind the students to be kind to the students who miss. Do not allow students to call other students "loser" or similar names. Remind the students that at some point everyone misses, so they all need to be supportive of others.

Standard 1	Standard 2	Standard 3	Standard 4	Standard 5	Standard 6
Skills and patterns	Learning concepts	Active participation	Physical fitness	Personal/social behavior	Active appreciation

Equipment Needs
Activity posters

What's Up! (Standards 1 & 4)

Appropriate for Grades 3-5

- Divide the students into pairs.

- Have the partners stand on opposite sides of the activity area.

- The students run to the center to perform an action with their partners and then return to their starting points.

- List the actions that the partners are supposed to perform on both sides of the activity area.

- Below are some examples of actions:
    o Give partner a high-five.
    o Touch the soles of the feet together.
    o Give partner a backward high-ten.
    o Jump around partner.
    o Form a tunnel for partner to crawl under.
    o Do a 360-degree jump turn with a high-five at the end.
    o Do a pinky swing (i.e., little fingers locked and move body in a circle).
    o Do a curl-up and finish with a high-five.
    o Do a tickle-ten (i.e., high-ten with fingers wiggling).
    o Give partner a low-five.
    o Give partner a jumping high-five and keep running to partner's starting point.

- Perform the activity three more times. During the next round, the pairs must perform each activity twice before returning to the sides of the activity area to see the next activity. During the third round, the pairs must perform each activity three times before returning to the sides of the activity area to see the next activity.

Cat Nips
The below adaptations address the additional standards indicated in the shaded boxes.

Standard 5: After the pairs perform an activity and congratulate each other on their performance, they switch partners and welcome their new partners.

Standard 1	Standard 2	Standard 3	Standard 4	Standard 5	Standard 6
Skills and patterns	Learning concepts	Active participation	Physical fitness	Personal/social behavior	Active appreciation

Roll and Run (Standards 1 & 4)

Equipment Needs
Task charts, dice, cones, balls

Appropriate for Grades 3-5

- Place task charts on the wall at the opposite end of the gym, away from the starting line.

- Divide the class into groups of four.

- Give each group a die and have each group stand by a cone on the starting line.

- The first student in each group rolls the die, runs to the task chart, and reads the skill that corresponds with the number he or she rolled.

- He or she then runs back to the group and leads the group in that task.

- After completing the first task, the next person rolls and runs.

- Continue this activity for a period of time.

- Below are some suggested tasks:

    o *Number 1*—Pretend to jump rope 20 times

    o *Number 2*—Perform 10 curl-ups

    o *Number 3*—Perform 10 push-ups

    o *Number 4*—Dribble a ball 25 times

    o *Number 5*—Run one lap

    o *Number 6*—Crab walk to the center of the gym

Cat Nips
The below adaptations address the additional standards indicated in the shaded boxes.

Standard 3: Have the students create six physical activities that could be done outside of the school day. Students should take these activities home and play them with a sibling or friend at least once during the week.

Standard 1	Standard 2	Standard 3	Standard 4	Standard 5	Standard 6
Skills and patterns	Learning concepts	Active participation	Physical fitness	Personal/social behavior	Active appreciation

Equipment Needs
Circuit signs, CD player, music, mat, Dynabands®

Boxer Circuit (Standards 1 & 4)

Appropriate for Grades 3-5

- Divide the students into pairs or groups of three.

- Place stations in a circle around the activity area. At each station, post a sign describing the specific activity for that station.

- Assign each group to a particular station and have them perform the activity at that station when the music starts.

- When the music stops, the students move clockwise to the next station.

- Below are some sample stations:

  o *Shadow boxing*—jab forward, backward, and side-to-side.

  o *Uppercut and squat*—throw two uppercuts while standing on the Dynabands®. Follow with a squat.

  o *Skipping*—jump rope.

  o *Punch and jab*—punch and jab with Dynabands® that are held from behind by the partner.

  o *Mirror*—walk fast around the activity area following the partner in an attempt to stay very close.

  o *Bob and weave*—move forward along a line while bobbing and weaving.

  o *Curl punch*—punch across the body while holding the Dynabands® under the feet.

  o *Jumps and punches*—jump up onto a folded mat and back down to the floor while throwing two punches.

  o *Coach's box*—find heart rate and rest.

Cat Nips
The below adaptations address the additional standards indicated in the shaded boxes.

Standard 2: In the coach's box, have the students determine their own target heart rate (THR) zone. The formula for finding a person's target heart rate zone is (220-age) × .65 (.85) = THR.

Standard 1	Standard 2	Standard 3	Standard 4	Standard 5	Standard 6
Skills and patterns	Learning concepts	Active participation	Physical fitness	Personal/social behavior	Active appreciation

CHAPTER 8

When Putting Cheese in the Mousetrap, Always Leave Room for the Mouse

Integration

All of the activities in this chapter meet Standard One (skills and patterns).
Use the "Gouda Ideas" to meet other standards.

Helpful Hints

Integration

- Integrating classroom content areas (e.g., math, reading, spelling) into the physical education classroom has become an essential and often required component of a physical education curriculum. Integration of classroom content areas is used to reinforce these content area concepts through the use of physical activity. Always remember that integration has great potential in a physical education program, but the main emphasis of physical education is on acquiring the knowledge and skills to maintain a healthy lifestyle. Remember too, "when putting cheese in the mousetrap, always leave room for the mouse."

- When introducing integration into physical activity, keep the concepts simple, with few rules. Try this as a measure: If the activity, drill, or game takes as long or longer to explain than to perform, then the integration is not worth the time.

- Find ways to adapt current drills and games for the introduction of integration.

- Students want to know the reasons for doing certain activities. While integration may be an outcome of an activity, make sure there is a reason for the activity.

A to Z Run (Standard 1)

Equipment Needs
CD player, music

Appropriate for Grades K-2

- Have the students find a spot in general space.

- When the music starts, the students perform the sequence below, starting with their left feet. When their right feet touch the floor, the students say a letter or a number.

1. March "A" to "Z"
2. Jog "A" to "Z"
3. March 1 to 20
4. Jog 1 to 20
5. March "A" to "Z"
6. March 1 to 20
7. Jog "A" to "Z"
8. Jog 1 to 20
9. March "A" to "Z"
10. March 1 to 20
11. March "A" to "Z"
12. Jog "A" to "Z"
13. Jog 1 to 20
14. Jog "A" to "Z"
15. March "A" to "Z"
16. Jog "A" to "Z"
17. March 1 to 20
18. Jog 1 to 20

Powered by Physical Education

Integration Connection
This activity allows for the integration of counting skills while allowing the students to remain active learners in physical skills.

Gouda Ideas
The below adaptations address the additional standards indicated in the shaded boxes.

Standard 2: Explain the concept of progression to the students. Each day, have students do three of the activities (#1-3, #4-6, #7-9, #10-12, #13-15, and #16-18) and then put two of the segments together (#1-6, #7-12, and #13-18). Finally, have the class do the entire sequence. Relate this activity to the concept of progression.

Standard 1	Standard 2	Standard 3	Standard 4	Standard 5	Standard 6
Skills and patterns	Learning concepts	Active participation	Physical fitness	Personal/social behavior	Active appreciation

Equipment Needs
Pictures, box, balls

Secrets of Life (Standard 1)

Appropriate for Grades K-2

• Put pictures of the secrets of life (i.e., sun, air, shelter, water, food) into a box (treasure chest).

• Tell the students that there are five secrets to life. Give them a brief opportunity to guess the secrets.

• Pull out a picture of the first secret and have the students do the activity associated with the secret.

• Below are the secret of life elements and their suggested activities:

    o *Sun*—stretch arms upward toward the sun.

    o *Air*—run in place very fast for 30 seconds, rest for five seconds, and then repeat.

    o *Shelter*—find a partner. One partner forms an inverted "V" shape and the other partner crawls through the inverted "V" shape 10 times. The partners then change positions.

    o *Water*—imitate swimming while moving across the activity area and back.

    o *Food*—bounce a ball 25 times in each corner of the activity area.

Powered by Physical Education

Integration Connection
This activity allows for the integration of environmental concepts while allowing the students to remain active learners in physical skills.

Gouda Ideas
The below adaptations address the additional standards indicated in the shaded boxes.

Standard 6: Have each student find a partner and create different activities for the secrets of life elements.

Standard 1	Standard 2	Standard 3	Standard 4	Standard 5	Standard 6
Skills and patterns	Learning concepts	Active participation	Physical fitness	Personal/social behavior	Active appreciation

Low and High (Standard 1)

Equipment Needs
Dice

Appropriate for Grades K-2

- Have each student find a partner. Each partner gets one die.

- Both students roll their die.

- The student who rolls the lowest number stays in place and jumps back and forth over a line. The student who rolls the higher of the two numbers does a teacher-specified activity (e.g., jog a lap, 10 karate kicks, six jumps and reaches, run and jump in the center circle, jump backward four times).

- Do the activity three times and tell the students that they have five seconds to find a new partner.

Powered by Physical Education

Integration Connection
This activity allows for the integration of math skills while allowing the students to remain active learners in physical skills.

Gouda Ideas
The below adaptations address the additional standards indicated in the shaded boxes.

Standard 5: If the partners roll the same number on their dice, show the students how to stand back-to-back to measure their height. If it is a "tall day," then the taller student stays in place, while the shorter student does the teacher-specified activity.

Standard 1	Standard 2	Standard 3	Standard 4	Standard 5	Standard 6
Skills and patterns	Learning concepts	Active participation	Physical fitness	Personal/social behavior	Active appreciation

Equipment Needs
Alphabet signs

Name Spelling (Standard 1)

Appropriate for Grades K-2

- Post laminated alphabet signs on the walls of the activity area.

- Have the students find a spot in general space.

- On a signal, have the students skip (or another locomotor skill) to the first letter of their names.

- The students touch the first letter of their respective names and then travel to the next letter until the students have completely spelled their names.

- When the students finish spelling their names, they return to their spots.

- Begin the activity again with a different locomotor skill. Add different spelling words if appropriate for the grade level.

Powered by
Physical
Education

Integration Connection
This activity allows for the integration of spelling skills while allowing the students to remain active learners in physical skills.

Gouda Ideas
The below adaptations address the additional standards indicated in the shaded boxes.

Standard 5: Have each student find a partner and travel together to spell both of the students' names before returning to their spots. Have the students decide whose name will be spelled first.

Standard 1	Standard 2	Standard 3	Standard 4	Standard 5	Standard 6
Skills and patterns	Learning concepts	Active participation	Physical fitness	Personal/social behavior	Active appreciation

Odds and Evens (Standard 1)

Equipment Needs
None

Appropriate for Grades 3-5

- Have each student find a partner.

- The partners line up facing each other on either side of the center line in the middle of the activity area.

- All students on one side are the "evens," while the students on the other side are the "odds" (see diagram below).

- The teacher calls out an even or odd number. The side that applies to the number called out chases the other side to their predetermined home line.

X = evens
O = odds

Powered by
Physical
Education

Integration Connection
This activity integrates the math concept of odds and evens while allowing the students to remain active learners in physical skills.

Gouda Ideas
The below adaptations address the additional standards indicated in the shaded boxes.

Standard 5: After playing the fleeing game three times, have the students on one side of the center line move to the next person in line. Have the new partners shake hands and say "good luck" or "thanks for playing."

Standard 1	Standard 2	Standard 3	Standard 4	Standard 5	Standard 6
Skills and patterns	Learning concepts	Active participation	Physical fitness	Personal/social behavior	Active appreciation

Equipment Needs
Note cards

Number Fun (Standard 1)

Appropriate for Grades 3-5

- As students enter the activity area, give them a numbered note card. Tell them that this will be their number for the day. More than one student should have each number.

- Using these numbers, the students can perform various activities:

    o Ask the students to find someone with the same number. The tallest student chooses what activity they perform.

    o Call out numbers and activities. For example, all number 3's skip and all number 6's gallop.

    o Use addition, subtraction, multiplication, or division. For example, tell the students to find a number that when added to theirs equals 10.

    o Ask the students to line up in numerical order (1 through 6). Have each line of six students perform 10 jumping jacks while holding hands.

    o Have the students get into groups of odd and even numbers. Give groups a different activity to perform.

    o Have each student find another number that is greater or lesser than his or her number. The higher or lower number chooses the activity the pair performs.

    o Have the students whose number is less than 6 slide and those whose number is greater than or equal to 6 skip.

Powered by Physical Education

Integration Connection
This activity allows for the integration of math skills while allowing the students to remain active learners in physical skills.

Gouda Ideas
The below adaptations address the additional standards indicated in the shaded boxes.

Standard 5: Remind the students to always thank their partners when they leave to perform a different activity.

Standard 1	Standard 2	Standard 3	Standard 4	Standard 5	Standard 6
Skills and patterns	Learning concepts	Active participation	Physical fitness	Personal/social behavior	Active appreciation

Coast to Coast (Standard 1)

Equipment Needs
Cardinal directional signs, balls, spot markers

Appropriate for Grades 3-5

- Label the walls of the activity area with signs indicating the cardinal directions (i.e., North, South, East, and West).

- Have the students each get a ball and spot marker and have them stand on their spot markers.

- State a pattern of cardinal directions. Have the students dribble over to touch the walls associated with the stated cardinal directions in the order the directions were stated. When they have completed the pattern, have the students return to their spot markers.

- State a new pattern of cardinal directions and begin the activity again.

- Below are some sample cardinal direction patterns:

  o North, South, East

  o South, North, West

  o West, East, North

  o North, South, North, South

  o West, North, South, East, West

  o West, East, North, South

Powered by Physical Education

Integration Connection
This activity allows for the integration of geographic cardinal directions while allowing the students to remain active learners in physical skills.

Gouda Ideas
The below adaptations address the additional standards indicated in the shaded boxes.

Standard 4: Include a ball-handling or fitness activity on each cardinal directional sign. When the students travel to a wall, they must complete the stated activity before moving on to next directional sign.

Standard 1	Standard 2	Standard 3	Standard 4	Standard 5	Standard 6
Skills and patterns	Learning concepts	Active participation	Physical fitness	Personal/social behavior	Active appreciation

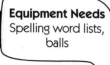

Equipment Needs
Spelling word lists, balls

Super Spellers (Standard 1)

Appropriate for Grades 3-5

- Have each student find a partner.

- Provide the students with a spelling list and make sure that each pair gets a ball.

- The students either pass or volley the ball to one another.

- With each pass or volley, the students say a letter of a word on the spelling list. This continues until they spell the word.

- Challenge the students to complete the spelling list in a specific amount of time.

Powered by Physical Education

Integration Connection
This activity assists in learning spelling words while allowing the students to remain active learners in physical skills.

Gouda Ideas
The below adaptations address the additional standards indicated in the shaded boxes.

Standard 4: Have the students run a lap after spelling each word.

Standard 1	Standard 2	Standard 3	Standard 4	Standard 5	Standard 6
Skills and patterns	Learning concepts	Active participation	Physical fitness	Personal/social behavior	Active appreciation

Card Shuffle (Standard 1)

Equipment Needs
Index cards,
CD player, music

Appropriate for Grades 3-5

- Divide the class into groups of two or three students.

- Each group gets a set of 12 index cards that have a number (from 1 to 12) on each card.

- When the music starts, have the students perform a teacher-specified activity (e.g., jogging, skipping, hopping).

- When the music stops, the teacher calls out a way for the groups to sort the cards.

- Below are some ways the cards can be sorted:

  o Put the cards in consecutive order from lowest to highest.
  o Put the cards in order from highest to lowest.
  o Put the odd cards in order and the even cards in order.
  o Make a rectangle from all the cards.

12 Activity Ideas
1 = Curl-ups
2 = Ski jumps
3 = Coffee grinder
4 = High knees
5 = V-sit
6 = Hop on right foot
7 = Hop on left foot
8 = Inch worm
9 = Frog jumps
10 = Pretend jump ropes
11 = Touch all four walls
12 = Crab walk

Powered by Physical Education

Integration Connection
This activity allows for the integration of the math skill of sorting while allowing the students to remain active learners in physical skills.

Gouda Ideas
The below adaptations address the additional standards indicated in the shaded boxes.

Standard 4: After completing the sorting activity, add an increased level of physical activity by calling out a number that is associated with an activity. The students quickly check the poster of activity ideas to see what extra activity they are supposed to do. Have them perform the activity until the music starts again. See the sample activity chart above.

Standard 1	Standard 2	Standard 3	Standard 4	Standard 5	Standard 6
Skills and patterns	Learning concepts	Active participation	Physical fitness	Personal/social behavior	Active appreciation

Equipment Needs
Deck of cards

Moving with Numbers (Standard 1)

Appropriate for Grades 3-5

- Give each student a playing card and have the students spread out around the room.

- Have each student quickly find a partner.

- The teacher tells the students to add up (subtract, multiply, or divide) the numbers on their cards and then perform the teacher-specified activity (e.g., jumping jacks, push-ups, curl-ups, touch that number of lines in the activity area) that many times.

- Give the students five seconds to find a new partner and begin the activity again.

Powered by Physical Education

Integration Connection
This activity allows for the integration of math skills while allowing the students to remain active learners in physical skills.

Gouda Ideas
The below adaptations address the additional standards indicated in the shaded boxes.

Standard 5: To further integrate math skills and to allow for social skill development, when the students find new partners have them stand back-to-back. In this back-to-back position, have them measure their heights to determine who is taller. The taller student must state an activity instead of using the teacher-specified activity.

Standard 1	Standard 2	Standard 3	Standard 4	Standard 5	Standard 6
Skills and patterns	Learning concepts	Active participation	Physical fitness	Personal/social behavior	Active appreciation

Show Me the Money (Standard 1)

Equipment Needs
Laminated play money, slips of paper

Appropriate for Grades 3-5

- Attach slips of paper that have fitness activities written on them to the back of laminated play money.

- Spread the money across the gym floor.

- Students work individually to try to accumulate "fitness" money.

- Each time a student picks up a piece of play money, he or she must perform the fitness activity indicated on the money in order to keep it. Stress that they must do the exercises correctly!

- After a set time, have the students stop and add up their money.

Powered by Physical Education

Integration Connection
This activity allows for the integration of math skills while allowing the students to remain active learners in physical skills.

Gouda Ideas
The below adaptations address the additional standards indicated in the shaded boxes.

Standard 2: At the end of the activity, ask the students which fitness activity should be worth the most money. By doing this, they are describing the difficulty of the various fitness activities.

Standard 5: Instead of completing this activity individually, pairs of students can perform the activity. Have them add their money together for a total collection.

Standard 5: Discuss with the students that it is good personal behavior to complete the activities listed on the back of the money.

Standard 1	Standard 2	Standard 3	Standard 4	Standard 5	Standard 6
Skills and patterns	Learning concepts	Active participation	Physical fitness	Personal/social behavior	Active appreciation

Equipment Needs
Math worksheets, pencils, numbered signs

Math-er-cise (Standard 1)

Appropriate for Grades 3-5

- In advance, prepare math worksheets appropriate for the age level of the class. Create worksheets that list questions in varying orders in order to eliminate having too many students at a station at one time. Post numbers that are answers to the questions on the walls of the gym. Establish a "math area" in which students can complete their calculations.

- Have each student find a partner.

- Using the worksheets, each pair determines the answer to one of the math problems in the math area.

- The pair leaves their pencil in the math area and runs to find the answer (number) posted on the gym wall. Once they find the number, both partners perform the corresponding exercise. For example, if the question is 20 minus 13, the pair runs to the number 7 posted on the wall. At the spot where number 7 is posted, there is a stated activity that the pair performs.

- After finishing the activity, the pair returns to the math area to answer the next question on their worksheet and the sequence begins again.

Powered by Physical Education

Integration Connection
This activity allows for the integration of math skills while allowing the students to remain active learners in physical skills.

Gouda Ideas
The below adaptations address the additional standards indicated in the shaded boxes.

Standard 5: Challenge the group to complete as many math problems as possible in three minutes. Suggest that it might be beneficial for the groups to help each other with difficult math problems.

Standard 1	Standard 2	Standard 3	Standard 4	Standard 5	Standard 6
Skills and patterns	Learning concepts	Active participation	Physical fitness	Personal/social behavior	Active appreciation

Equipment Needs
Jump ropes or
elastic bands

Human Polygon (Standard 1)

Appropriate for Grades 3-5

- Call out the name of a polygon (e.g., hexagon, heptagon, octagon, pentathlon, square, parallelogram, quadrilateral).

- The students gather in groups that represent the number of sides the polygon has. For example, if a square is called, students should form groups of four.

- The students use their bodies to create the stated polygon shape.

- *Option*: The students may use jump ropes or elastic bands to form a shape.

Powered by
Physical
Education

Integration Connection
This activity allows for the integration of math concepts associated with the number of sides in a mathematical design while allowing the students to remain active learners in physical skills.

Gouda Ideas
The below adaptations address the additional standards indicated in the shaded boxes.

Standard 4: Add more physical activity by having the students do a specified activity once for every side the polygon has. For example, if the polygon is a square, the students would do four of the stated activity (e.g., laps, jumping jacks, push-ups).

Standard 1	Standard 2	Standard 3	Standard 4	Standard 5	Standard 6
Skills and patterns	Learning concepts	Active participation	Physical fitness	Personal/social behavior	Active appreciation

Equipment Needs
Foam noodles,
rubber chickens,
rubber fish

Dinosaur Tag (Standard 1)

Appropriate for Grades 3-5

- Set boundaries for a tag game.

- Select several students to be taggers and assign them different dinosaurs names. Each dinosaur has a different method of tagging other students. For example, a T-Rex can only tag someone who is moving; Raptors can only jump around to tag others; an Ankylosaurus must tag using a foam noodle; a Diplodocus can only walk around to tag others; a Pteranodon must tag others with a rubber chicken; and a Plesiosaur must tag using a rubber fish.

- Assign at least two students to be Stegosaurus.

- Once a student is tagged by a dinosaur (other than a Stegosaurus), he or she must move around like a dinosaur until saved by a Stegosaurus. Once the tagged student is saved, he or she can rejoin the game.

Powered by
Physical
Education

Integration Connection
This activity allows for the integration of
the science concept of dinosaurs while
allowing the students to remain active
learners in physical skills.

Gouda Ideas
The below adaptations address the additional standards indicated in the shaded boxes.

Standard 2: Have the students identify the force of dinosaur movements. Allow them to demonstrate the heaviest of these movements.

Standard 1	Standard 2	Standard 3	Standard 4	Standard 5	Standard 6
Skills and patterns	Learning concepts	Active participation	Physical fitness	Personal/social behavior	Active appreciation

Scrabble (Standard 1)

Equipment Needs
Pencils, paper, letter cards

Appropriate for Grades 3-5

- Divide the class into groups of two to three students.

- Give each group a pencil and paper.

- Define the boundaries of the playing area and place the groups along the outer perimeter of the area. In the middle of the playing area, spread out letter cards that have a letter on each card. Using the cards, make several sets of the alphabet. To make the activity easier, cards can be face up.

- On a signal, group members travel as the teacher specifies (e.g., hopping, skipping), one at time, to the middle of the activity area to collect a letter card.

- As the group members bring back their letter cards, the groups try to form words.

- Once a team has formed a word (they do not have to use all the letters they have), the teacher should verify that the word is a real word. Once verified, the group writes the word on their paper and returns the letters to the center pile.

  - The group continues to collect cards to form other words.

  - Groups attempt to form as many words as possible in the allotted time.

Powered by Physical Education

Integration Connection
This activity allows for the integration of math concepts associated with the number of sides in a mathematical design.

Gouda Ideas
The below adaptations address the additional standards indicated in the shaded boxes.

Standard 5: Remind students to take only one letter card on each trip.

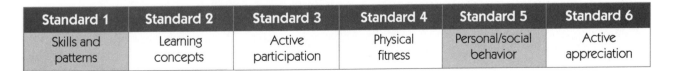

Standard 1	Standard 2	Standard 3	Standard 4	Standard 5	Standard 6
Skills and patterns	Learning concepts	Active participation	Physical fitness	Personal/social behavior	Active appreciation

Equipment Needs
Arm bands or
handkerchiefs,
spelling word lists

Spelling Tag (Standard 1)

Appropriate for Grades 3-5

- Designate two to four students to be taggers depending on the class size. Give each tagger an arm band or handkerchief to wear. Also designate two to four students to be spell checkers. There should be enough spell checkers to keep the game moving. Give each spell checker a list of spelling words.

- When a student is tagged by a tagger, he or she begins jumping up and down while reciting the alphabet.

- Spell checkers move quickly to any jumpers. A spell checker will give the jumper a word to spell. After spelling the word correctly, the jumper may re-enter the game.

- Change the taggers and spell checkers often.

Powered by
Physical
Education

Integration Connection
This activity works on spelling words
while allowing the students to remain
active learners in physical skills

Gouda Ideas
The below adaptations address the additional standards indicated in the shaded boxes.

Standard 3: Send a list of spelling words related to physical activity home with every student. Pair these words with an activity. Have the students ask a family member to check their spelling and do the physical activity with them.

Standard 1	Standard 2	Standard 3	Standard 4	Standard 5	Standard 6
Skills and patterns	Learning concepts	Active participation	Physical fitness	Personal/social behavior	Active appreciation

Bouncing Numbers (Standard 1)

Equipment Needs
Balls

Appropriate for Grades 3-5

- Students count to 100 by 2's while dribbling a ball. Whenever the ball touches the ground they say the number.

- Repeat the activity counting by 3's, 5's, and 10's.

Powered by Physical Education

Integration Connection
This activity allows for the integration of math skills while allowing the students to remain active learners in physical skills.

Gouda Ideas
The below adaptations address the additional standards indicated in the shaded boxes.

Standard 5: Instead of completing this activity individually, the students could practice bounce passes to each other using the same counting process.

Standard 1	Standard 2	Standard 3	Standard 4	Standard 5	Standard 6
Skills and patterns	Learning concepts	Active participation	Physical fitness	Personal/social behavior	Active appreciation

Equipment Needs
Dice, graph paper, probability chart, pencils, task sheets

Partner Probability (Standard 1)

Appropriate for Grades 3-5

- Have each student find a partner.

- Give each pair a set of dice, graph paper, a probability chart, a pencil, and a task sheet. A sample probability chart, which can also be created on graph paper, is on page 187.

- The first partner rolls the dice, adds the total of the dice together, and performs the activity on the task sheet that corresponds to the number (a sample task sheet is on page 187).

- While the first partner performs the activity, the other partner places a checkmark on the probability chart, below the number rolled and in the Trial 1 row.

- The partners then change roles.

- After a period of time, have the pairs add up the total number of times each number was rolled. Have the pairs create a graph, using graph paper, to chart the frequency a number was rolled and shade in the graph.

- Have the pairs compare graphs and discuss their results.

Powered by Physical Education

Integration Connection
This activity allows for the integration of the math skill of probability while allowing the students to remain active learners in physical skills.

Gouda Ideas
The below adaptations address the additional standards indicated in the shaded boxes.

Standard 3: Have the students take a copy of the probability chart and task sheet home to demonstrate their skills and predictions to family members.

Standard 1	Standard 2	Standard 3	Standard 4	Standard 5	Standard 6
Skills and patterns	Learning concepts	Active participation	Physical fitness	Personal/social behavior	Active appreciation

Probability Chart

Physical Activity and Probability Trials

Number on Dice

Trial	2	3	4	5	6	7	8	9	10	11	12
1											
2											
3											
4											
5											
6											
7											
8											
9											
10											
11											
12											
13											
14											
15											
16											
17											
18											

Task Sheet

Number	Activity
2	Skip 1 lap
3	10 push-ups
4	10 crunches
5	Calf stretch (both legs)
6	Give 4 high five's
7	360 jumps – 3 times
8	10 side-to-side jumps
9	10 jump and claps
10	5 jumping jacks
11	Do-si-do 2 people
12	5 pretend jump shots

ABOUT THE AUTHORS

Joella Mehrhof is a Professor in the Department of Health, Physical Education, and Recreation at Emporia State University in Emporia, Kansas. Dr. Mehrhof teaches elementary physical education methods, dance/rhythms methods, and several different graduate level courses. She has professionally served in national, regional, and state leadership positions and has authored 13 books and several journal articles.

Kathy Ermler is a well-known presenter in the physical education field. Dr. Ermler has received numerous grants and assisted several school districts in their efforts to secure PEP grants. She has authored numerous books and journal articles and has served in a variety of professional leadership roles. Presently she is Chair and Professor in the Department of Health, Physical Education, and Recreation at Emporia State University.

Vicki Worrell has presented at numerous national and international workshops and conferences. Dr. Worrell is a NASPE National Elementary Physical Educator of the Year and is the 2006 NASPE Joy of Effort recipient. She teaches elementary physical education methods for both classroom teachers and physical education majors as an Associate Professor at Emporia State University.

Joan Brewer is an Assistant Professor in the Department of Health, Physical Education, and Recreation at Emporia State University. She is the recipient of numerous professional awards including the AAHPERD Mabel Lee Award. Dr. Brewer teaches secondary physical education methods, as well as several other wellness and physical education courses.

RESOURCES

Published by the National Association for Sport and Physical Education
for quality physical education programs:

Moving into the Future: National Standards for Physical Education, 2nd Edition (2004), Stock No. 304-10275

Quality Coaches, Quality Sports: National Standards for Sport Coaches, 2nd Edition (2006), Stock No. 304-10274

Roadblocks to Quality Physical Education (2007), Stock No. 304-10323

2006 Shape of the Nation Report: Status of Physical Education in the USA (2006), Stock No. 304-10331

Movement-Based Learning: Academic Concepts and Physical Activity for Ages Three through Eight (2006), Stock No. 304-10300

Physical Educators' Guide to Successful Grant Writing (2005), Stock No. 304-10291

Physical Activity for Children: A Statement of Guidelines (2004), Stock No. 304-10276

On Your Mark… Get Set… Go!: A Guide for Beginning Physical Education Teachers (2004), Stock No. 304-10264

Concepts and Principles of Physical Education: What Every Student Needs to Know (2003), Stock No. 304-10261

Beyond Activities: Elementary Volume (2003), Stock No. 304-10265

Beyond Activities: Secondary Volume (2003), Stock No. 304-10268

National Standards for Beginning Physical Education Teachers (2003), Stock No. 304-10273

Active Start: A Statement of Physical Activity Guidelines for Children Birth to Five Years (2002), Stock No. 304-10254

Appropriate Practice Documents

Appropriate Practice in Movement Programs for Young Children, (2000), Stock No. 304-10232

Appropriate Practices for Elementary School Physical Education (2000), Stock No. 304-10230

Appropriate Practices for Middle School Physical Education (2001), Stock No. 304-10248

Appropriate Practices for High School Physical Education (2004), Stock No. 304-10272

Opportunity to Learn Documents

Opportunity to Learn Standards for Elementary Physical Education (2000), Stock No. 304-10242

Opportunity to Learn Standards for Middle School Physical Education (2004), Stock No. 304-10290

Opportunity to Learn Standards for High School Physical Education (2004), Stock No. 304-10289

Assessment Series

Assessing Gymnastics in Elementary School Physical Education (2007), Stock No. 304-10303

Assessment of Swimming in Physical Education (2005), Stock No. 304-10301

Assessing Dance in Elementary Physical Education (2005), Stock No. 304-10304

Assessing Concepts: Secondary Biomechanics (2003), Stock No. 304-10220

Assessment in Outdoor Adventure Physical Education (2003), Stock No. 304-10218

Assessing Student Outcomes in Sport Education (2003), Stock No. 304-10219

Assessing Heart Rate in Physical Education (2002), Stock No. 304-10214

Authentic Assessment of Physical Activity for High School Students (2002), Stock No. 304-10216

Portfolio Assessment for K-12 Physical Education (2000), Stock No. 304-10213

Elementary Heart Health: Lessons and Assessment (2001), Stock No. 304-10215

Standards-Based Assessment of Student Learning: A Comprehensive Approach (1999), Stock No. 304-10206

Assessment in Games Teaching (1999), Stock No. 304-10212

Assessing Motor Skills in Elementary Physical Education (1999), Stock No. 304-10207

Creating Rubrics for Physical Education (1999), Stock No. 304-10209

Order online at www.naspeinfo.org or call 1-800-321-0789
Shipping and handling additional.

National Association for Sport and Physical Education, an association of the American Alliance for Health, Physical Education, Recreation, and Dance, 1900 Association Drive, Reston, VA 20191, naspe@aahperd.org, 703-476-3410